ESSAYS / TRUE STORIES / VIGNETTES

RUSSELL HILL

GHOST TROUT

*The search for a rare trout and other essays, including
a dance by the daughter of California poet Joaquin Miller.*

PLEASUREBOATSTUDIO
A NONPROFIT LITERARY PRESS

ISBN 978-0-912887-89-0
Library of Congress Control Number:
2019951257

Cover photograph by Russell Hill
Cover and book Design by Lauren Grosskopf

Pleasure Boat Studio books are available through your favorite bookstore
and through the following:
SPD (Small Press Distribution) 800-869-7553
Baker & Taylor 800-775-1100
Ingram 615-793-5000
Amazon.com and bn.com

& through
PLEASURE BOAT STUDIO: A NONPROFIT LITERARY PRESS
WWW.PLEASUREBOATSTUDIO.COM
Seattle, Washington

for Ronald and Paul

*There are only two or three human stories,
and they go onrepeating themselves as fiercely
as if they had never happened before.*

-Willa Cather. *O Pioneers*

GHOST
TROUT

Contents

I
Fragments

MEMORY, BITS AND PIECES, and the threads that connect those pieces are often woven through other fragments. It is like a ragged sweater; if you pull on one piece of hanging yarn, somewhere else in the sweater the weave bunches, pulled tight, or perhaps a different sleeve begins to unravel. Once we had a dog that grew old and deaf and nearly blind and began to lash out at people who came near him, assuming that anything unseen or unheard was a threat, and then his hips began to give out and one afternoon I found him dragging himself across the floor, unable to stand on four legs. The vet said that he was unraveling. I can stitch him up, he said, but something else will come apart. You won't do him any favor by tying up the loose ends.

I came down across the meadow in the half dark and the grass beneath my feet was suddenly no longer soft. The temperature had dipped below freezing and the wet grass crunched and I knew that I would have to wade the creek and I wanted to get there before it was too black to see where the water began.

And so the black dog that I had to put down is stitched to other fragments, black threads that span half a century.

A place in my childhood. Woods beyond the fields that were on my Uncle Earl's farm. They were filled with birds, mostly crows. Sometimes in the evening they came in a great cloud and spiraled down into the trees as if the trees breathed them in and they shouted at each other and it grew dark and I could hear the cicadas begin their constant whine that would last all night. I followed the rows of corn back up to the farmhouse, the narrow aisles of corn high over my head. The leaves were sharp and I held my hands in front of my face and it seemed much longer than when I had come down to the woods. There was a creek at the edge of the woods. It was no more than a trickle in the summer, but the water was cold and once I took my clothes off and lay in the water. It was not deep enough to cover my body.

We are all a collection of our childhood. Dog-eared scrapbooks filled with the things that shape us.

I'm remembering a feather I found under those trees. The feather was black satin and the quill was transparent where it had been attached to the wing, ivory as it grew thinner in the rising fan. Light as a feather. It had no weight in my hand, only the soft touch against my palm. There is no weight to what I remember of that summer. It is all rising heat and chaff that floats in the sun.

A fox crossed the road. It came out of the woods onto the pavement and at first I thought it was a cat or a small dog but the sun caught its coat and it was a sudden burst of flame and it stopped, looked at me, and then it was gone in the brush on the far side of the road. It came out of the wood and crossed into a field. The field had huge rolls of hay and it was near Villenueve. I wanted to walk and it was hot and I wanted to get in the car and drive to the sea. If I had gone to the sea I would not have seen the fox.

The sun slanted across the pocket valley toward the wall of pines. The creek bubbled softly through the meadow and the cattle were far off. A larger shape that appeared to be a bull stood still, not grazing. At the far edge of the meadow, just before the trees, there was a line of lime green where the spring line faded to a rich yellow as the grass came toward me. I watched the water turn dark, waiting for a big brown trout to begin feeding but there was nothing, only the iridescent blue of damsel flies hovering where the damp grass dragged in the water and the sucking of water over stones. The silence was complete.

An egret rowed along the edge of the road earlier, paralleling the road, its neck bent in an S, the wings like oars parting the air, a sharp white against the intense green of the rice field. I slowed to see how fast it was moving but it veered off, and I stopped and watched until I could no longer see it.

There is a picture of me and Ronald in front of the little house in Wyanet. I am blowing out the candles of my second birthday cake. I wear a white blouse and white shorts. I have a full head of curly blonde hair. I could have been mistaken as Ronald's little sister. Ronald has on American flag socks with red, white and blue stripes and stars around the top. The house was tiny. Two rooms and a kitchen. I thought it was on the other side of the railroad tracks, but Paul said no, it wasn't just on the other side—it was next to the tracks and when an Illinois Burlington freight train came past, the house vibrated. Paul will be born a year after that photograph was taken. There is another memory of that house. It was a hot, Midwestern afternoon, and I ran naked into the street where other naked children cavorted. They filled buckets of water from a standpipe and hurled the water at each other. They were, I was told later, Kentuckians. They were the ones in the front row of the school picture with Ronald in it. They sat, cross-legged on the ground, wearing bib overalls, all of them barefoot. Ronald stands at the end of the second row, wearing long trousers, a white shirt and a tie. He must have been about ten. When I ran naked into the street, my mother came out and pulled me back inside. It was my mother's sense of decorum, an innate sense of dignity that took me from the shouting group of naked children. We were not Kentuckians, whatever that meant. We did not run naked in the street, no matter what our age. My older brother wore a tie for the annual school picture. He was the odd one out, and for the rest of his life he would be the odd one out, the boy wearing the tie, the man wearing a three piece suit and a Homburg hat long after other men had discarded their hats and vests.

I do not think I invented the naked children in the dirt street running in the mud they made on a hot afternoon. How else could they have become a part of my memory unless I witnessed them? It was not a scene that would have been told to me. Where, in my brain, was that scene stored? In some white envelope that had written on it: do not open until you are an old man.

We moved to a house owned by a retired Methodist minister, who shared his house with us. It wasn't far from my grandfather's house. Apparently he didn't approve of my father, who by now was working as a carpenter, and we were not invited to share his large Victorian home. I remember nothing of the Reverend's house except that next to the driveway there were hollyhocks, and I could make little dolls out of the blossoms. Tear off the round bud and put it on the stem of the blossom and I had what looked like a tiny woman in a ball gown with no arms, and no features.

And then we moved to Elgin.

That was a narrow house and my father's mother came to live with us. She had a bad heart and spent much of her time in bed, a large woman who was folded into the feather mattress. I tried following my older brother around. He called me "shadow," and he and his friends would let me tag along until we were some distance from the house, in an unfamiliar neighborhood and then they would suddenly split up, confusing me, and I would be left to find my way home. I was in second grade, and my teacher, Miss Higganbothan, had us memorize poems. I memorized a poem that began, "The woodpecker pecked out a little round hole, and made him a house in the telephone pole."

I recited it for mothers who came to the school, but my mother wasn't there. She worked at the Elgin watch factory, which, because the war was on, had switched over to making instruments, including bomb sights for airplanes. My father worked as a draughtsman at the Seneca shipyard where LST's were made that the Chicago Bridge and Iron Works launched sideways into the Illinois River. We went once to a launching and sat on the opposite shore. But we sat among poison ivy and Ronald and I came down with severe cases on our ankles where our trousers and socks had not protected us. The cure for the blisters that rose and opened, draining fluid, itching like fire, was to submerge our feet and ankles in a mixture of acetic acid and water. The pain was excruciating. I remember screaming as Ronald held my leg in the bucket. I do not remember him howling with pain. He was stoic even though he would have been no more than eleven years old at the time. What I did not realize was that he was different. He knew things I did not know.

He knew that my father was blind in one eye, a fact I did not discover until I was nearly fifty years old. My father had a glass eye, the result of an accident in which he had plunged through the windshield of a truck. I was told, years later, that he was lucky to have survived the crash, and there was speculation that he would lose both eyes. But I wasn't privy to that information; I only knew that we lived a solitary life in a little house in Elgin where my grandmother died. I do not remember that event. Suddenly she was not there. I do not remember grief or tears or anything other than the fact that the feather bed was empty and we would move again. I lived in a family in which emotions were not worn on the sleeve. They were not even worn in the pocket. I do not ever remember anyone crying at someone's death, except, perhaps when my older brother cried at my father's funeral. I was startled at his behavior, as if it were not appropriate, out of character for him and the family, and the moment passed quickly.

And so I carried those scenes from my childhood somewhere in my head, and there was no one I could share them with. We were not a family that shared secrets. We were not a family that shared any kind of emotional baggage. The disappearance of a grandmother, an empty bed, and no memory of a funeral or a ceremony or grief that she had ceased to exist.

The woodpecker pecked out a little round hole. That much I remember.

We lived for a short while in an apartment in Elgin and then moved to 123 S. Mitchell Street in Arlington Heights in 1943, the sixth house we would occupy in eight years. My father always worked, even in the worst depression years, and now he had a job as a high school teacher and basketball coach. But the following spring when they tested teachers for tuberculosis, his world fell apart. What is strange is that I don't remember him leaving us. His letter of resignation to the school board was accepted nearly on April Fool's Day in 1945.

I went to grade school in Arlington Heights. I assume Paul did, too. Ronald? I don't even remember him living in the same house with us. We had a dog, a cocker spaniel that ran into the snow and when it came inside, ice clung between the pads of its paws and had to be plucked out. The dog cried every time. Once, I remember crossing a vacant lot on the way to school. It was covered with new snow and there was a scarlet tanager on a leafless bush in the center of it. I remember that red. It was like a clot of blood in a whiteness so brilliant that it hurt my eyes.

The school was a two story brick building, a block that resembled an impregnable fortress. High double-hung windows filled the walls of the classrooms. I remember snow gliding past those windows, finding myself outside the glass, the flakes clinging to my hair and the teacher suddenly calling my name, bringing me back into the classroom with a jolt. I often drifted away from the lessons.

There was a basement in our house with a coal bin and an ice man stopped in front to deliver ice. We waited until he was inside the house to climb into the back of the truck and pick up slivers of ice to suck. And then my father went off to the magic mountain and we left Arlington Heights. Only one other event stays with me: Paul and I hiked out to Arlington Park, the race track that was just outside the town. Somehow, we thought it would be an easy walk. We made sandwiches, a piece of bread and a slice of cheese and we walked through the fields. The corn had been harvested and the stubs of corn stalks cut at our ankles. It took several hours to get to the racetrack, a huge, cavernous structure that was closed because of the war. Its emptiness was frightening and we immediately turned around to come back. It began to get dark, the temperature dropping below freezing. I do not remember if I was frightened at that point or not. I only wanted to keep Paul walking. Our shoes grew heavy with frozen mud and when we finally sighted the lights of the houses at the edge of town I was relieved. Once we were on a street, a police car found us and took us home. I must have been in trouble for taking my six year old brother off across the frozen fields, but not much was said. Nothing much was ever said. The words were swallowed in our house.

I fell and broke a bone in my ankle and now I'm wearing a heavy boot that immobilizes the joint. It was the fall of an old man, a senseless tumble, since my foot had fallen asleep and when I stood it did not function. So I sat in the waiting room at the doctor's office and I thought, I'm in a room full of old people, and then it dawned on me that I was one of those old people. That face I see in the mirror is not a familiar face, bags under the eyes, lines on the cheeks, the face of an old man.

Henning Mankell, writing in *Quicksand, What it means to be a human being,* writes: "over the years what one looks like in the mirror changes, but behind that mirror image is always the real you."

Here I am, writing once again, putting words on paper. I am trying to make sense of something, but I'm not sure what. Sense of my life? Sense of being alive? Sense of what I did for eighty-three years? I have included among these essays dogs, people I remember, places, streams and rivers, birds, my parents, brothers, food, storms, rain, words, moments in the classroom, bits and pieces.

Among the first words of *Ghost Trout,* I wrote: "Memory, bits and pieces, and the threads that connect those pieces are often woven through other fragments. It is like a ragged sweater; if you pull on one piece of hanging yarn, somewhere else in the sweater the weave bunches, pulled tight, or perhaps a different sleeve begins to unravel."

I wrote that ten years ago. So I pull at the threads, jotting down the bits and pieces, sometimes in the coffee shop on the corner, sometimes in the small hours of the morning here at my keyboard. They come floating back and as I write, I try to give them some shape. It is in shaping them that I remember more clearly. Something else that Mankell wrote:

"Nobody wants to be forgotten but nearly everybody is."

The only people left who remember Aunt Edna and Uncle Howard standing in Mr. Frye's tomato field are my brother Paul and I. And when we are gone, they, too, will be gone. There will be no one to remember Uncle Howard talking to Mr. Frye, his way of avoiding the work of picking tomatoes, no one to remember Aunt Edna bending over, selecting the biggest, ripest tomatoes that she could spend the next week canning. No one to remember the smell in her kitchen as she made chili sauce and fried big slices of beef-steak tomatoes coated with egg and cracker crumbs in but-ter, melting cheese on top. And when the two of us are gone, there will be no one who will remember our games of catch or throwing snowballs in the vacant lot next to 123 S. Mitchell Street.

Auden, in the final lines of the film *Night Mail,* wrote, as the train pulled into the vast empty station at Edinburgh, "for who can bear to be forgot."

But Mankell is right. My father and mother will be forgot-ten when Paul and I are no longer here to conjure up mem-ories of them. My father, squatting in the Victory garden in Arlington Heights is a dim figure. Anyone seeing that photo-graph will wonder who he was. I can remember his slender figure, his quiet reserve, and what must have been his stark emptiness when he got off the train at Valmora in the New Mexico emptiness. Who can remember when every family had a member suffering with tuberculosis?

So I keep pulling at the threads. I have pulled at several here. In the following pages I will pull more of them.

ONE NIGHT I DROVE WEST from 73rd Street toward the bay and when I ran out of industrial buildings I suddenly came on a roadway covered with toads. Some secret signal had caused them to migrate and I was driving over a carpet of creatures that turned the road into a swirling mass of living things. And then they were gone.

Night time creatures. Possums crossing the road, their long pink tails like giant rats, scurrying in the dark toward some house where the skirt revealed an opening in the foundation, a chance to find some warmth in a dark place.

IT IS OCTOBER on the North Fork of the Yuba and the river rushes, low, a quiet whisper at night. There is an earthen bench high on one bank where an old apple tree bends toward the river and in the weeds below it are windfall apples, gnarled little things like the fists of a child, but they are sharp and sweet and the leaves of the aspens float in the afternoon breeze, gold coins that drift toward the water. I sit on that bench and have a scotch, warm brown liquid that burns my throat and I watch the riffle that foams over a granite slab, imagine a trout drifting in the current, waiting for some late insect to tumble toward it.

Earlier that afternoon in a quiet backwater a water ouzel dipped into the pool above me. A soft grey bird, it suddenly went under the water and I knew that it was wading on the bottom, looking for a hellgrammite or the pupae of a stone fly and suddenly it popped up, not ten feet from me and went under again. It was John Muir's dipper, the bird he described on his journey to Yosemite a century before. It was a magic weekend, filled with light and dark and a bright trout not eight inches long that came to a fly in the shadow of a rock and I no longer cared if I caught anything else. I watched the long back cast and waited, held my breath and there was a moon that rose over the river and a blue flame in the wall of the little cabin where I slept. It popped on periodically during the night and each time I heard it, I waited while it flared, and then I slept again.

Art Morris and I slept in a cabin named *Trout*. We sat on the little porch in the heat of the afternoon, drinking a cold beer and waiting for the sun to go off the water, the temperature to drop and the fish to rise.

On another hot afternoon I sat in the cool front porch of the Harrington farmhouse outside of Wyanet. It was a square, two story house, a heavy block that faced the north and endless corn fields. The porch covered the front of the house, deep, with sturdy columns and a slanted floor. Nobody used that porch. Everybody came into the house by the door at the back, next to the kitchen. They came through the gate beside the stock tank, just beneath the windmill, crossed the green lawn and opened the screen door next to the small room that housed the milk separator.

The front door led into the parlor, a room with shades drawn, smelling of furniture polish and dust. I must have been about twelve years old. We had come back to Illinois to visit and Paul and I had spent the day chasing piglets. My mother's cousin, Howard Brieser, farmed his father-in-laws' acreage, and that day he had been castrating piglets. Paul and I ran after them, tackling them against the fence, dragging them to where Howard and a neighbor farmer sat with their sharp pocket knives.

Work stopped in the heat of the afternoon and somewhere in the house Howard napped while Aunt Blanche, his mother-in-law, began preparation for dinner in the summer kitchen, a screened-in addition at the back of the farmhouse. I sat on that shady porch and looked at the shimmering air across the road.

That same shimmering air hovered over the LaPorte road on a September afternoon forty years later. Art and I climbed out of Nelson Creek, having fished it all morning, taking bright trout from the shaded canyon stream. And now we sat on the edge of the gravel road, looking across into the haze that filled the Middle Fork canyon like faint blue smoke.

Art is gone and I fish rivers that are more accessible to a man my age. October light, John Gardner called it. Aspens are bright splotches of gold against the dark green firs. The North Fork of the Yuba is low and translucent green. Tires rumble on the bridge that crosses above Downieville. In another few weeks the first snow will come, the flakes dissolving in the black water, rounded white caps appearing on the rocks, and the cabins will be boarded up for the winter. In the Central Valley the rain will fall steadily, the rice fields will fill with water and snow geese will blanket the edges of the highway.

Alexander von Humboldt never saw the ghost trout that is named after him. He never sailed in the current that sweeps down from Alaska, bearing his name. He never waded into the Humboldt River or saw the red-winged blackbirds that swarm in the reeds along its banks. He didn't see the solitary egret that stalks the damp headwater near Deeth.

In the high alkaline desert of Nevada, forty miles northeast of Elko, the sagebrush is darkening and the temperature has dropped close to freezing. The Humboldt cutthroat trout will winter in those ice-edged streams, just as they have learned to adapt to the summer inferno that raises the temperature to the point where no other trout can survive.

The towering ridges of the Ruby Mountains are still bathed in soft light.

October light.

II
Ghost Trout

IN MID-OCTOBER I drove to Truckee, spent the morning on Sagehen Creek and then, as clouds began to tower over the mountains, thought of going on to Reno and beyond to Elko. I stopped in Truckee and called the number I had been given for the ranch foreman near Wildcat Creek north of Deeth. I explained who I was and asked if the storm that seemed to be coming from the east had passed over him.

"Yesterday," he said. "It was a toad drownder. A real gully washer. That creek and every other draw is belly-high. It'll go down by tonight but the creek is gonna be chocolate for a while."

"So coming out there to fish for trout isn't a good idea?"

"Suit yourself, young man."

"I wouldn't be there until tomorrow, maybe the day after."

"Like I said, suit yourself. Where you at now?"

"Truckee, over in California."

"Long way," he said. "They aren't very big, you know."

"I know that. I just want to see one, hold it in my hand."

Long pause. Outside the phone booth the first drops were splattering on the pavement, big thundershower drops, accompanied by long crackling rollers.

"It's probably not the same storm," I said.

"This one went south, over into the Rubies."

The Ruby Mountains, south and east of Elko glow in the late afternoon, rise like the faint wash of a Japanese woodcut.

"But you think the weather will clear?"

"This is October, young man," he said. I resisted the impulse to tell him that I was nearing my seventieth birthday. "You come on over here and it's gonna be colder than a witch's tit when the sun goes down. But you're welcome to it."

I decided against the long drive. I drove out to Martis Lake and watched the rain dot the surface, every once in a while the sky lit by a flash of lightning. A movement among the reeds caught my eye and I rolled down the window. There was a heron at the edge of the lake, not ten yards off. It was wet, bedraggled, its neck thin with the feathers plastered to it and its head not much more than a bony protrusion. It cocked its head at me and hunched its shoulders ever so slightly, and then, as if they had sprung from its body, the huge wings unfolded and the bird rose, the rich blue of its wings in sharp contrast to the wet gray of its body, only to settle again not far off, turning its head so it could fix one eye on me. The rain came horizontally now, borne by a sharp wind across the lake.

There was a bottle of scotch in the back of the truck and I knew that I would get wet trying to find it but I went around to the back of the truck anyway, lifted the lid of the camper shell and rummaged among the jumble of fishing rods and clothes until I unearthed the bottle and a glass. Back in the cab, the windows steamed up as I sat there, my sweater damp from the rain, my hair wet; I poured a shot into the glass and listened to the rain drum on the roof of the cab. When the storm slacked off I drove back to I-80 and headed home. The steelhead would start to move with these first Fall storms. I would leave the Humboldt cutt until the Spring.

DEETH O'NEIL ROAD. At five o'clock sleep was impossible. Eighteen wheelers were firing up all around me and I remembered the night before when I had gone to the counter at the truck stop and asked, "Can I park my rig here tonight?"

He looked at me and said, "And just what kind of a 'rig' are we talking about here?" Obviously there was something suspect about me.

"It's a Ford Explorer," I said, and he shook his head. "You're welcome to park, but I want you to park it way off where you won't get squashed in the dark."

And now, as the outline of the Ruby Mountains to the south began to form, the big rig truckers were starting their engines and moving out. I pulled on my pants and went into the truck stop where I bought a ham and cheese sandwich and a couple of bottles of water and a plastic-wrapped sausage and egg sandwich. A half hour later I was at the Deeth turnoff.

Deeth. Three abandoned houses and a ten-wide with a flagpole and DEETH POST OFFICE on the side. A railroad siding with a dozen wrecked Union Pacific railroad cars, twisted and scorched. Two roads go north. The second is the O'Neil-Deeth County Road. The map shows a thin brown line, as if someone drew it with a straight ruler, twenty-one miles of dirt road before it jogs left, then right and thirty-eight miles until it crosses Current Creek. Just outside of Deeth the road threads through a marsh and birds whip up in front of the truck: a willet, sharp contrast between the white and black on the wings, a black-necked stilt, delicate with its pencil-thin neck, a snipe. Meadowlarks trill and a flock of crows rises, yelling at my intrusion.

Then the road settles, a packed dirt surface that runs straight north, the tires of the Ford humming, the truck vibrating, periodically slamming through a pot hole or a washout. The sky is dark, heavy, and there is rain ahead of me, clouds clinging to the far off mountains.

There are no fences, no telephone poles, only the sagebrush and once, ten miles in, a pointless cattle guard across the road.

At sixteen miles I am startled to see what looks like a figure far ahead, something erect beside the road and it looks like the figure of a human being. As it gets closer it appears to be a man, standing beside the road, hitchhiking and I think, holy shit, what the fuck is somebody doing out here, early in the morning, miles from any living thing. I slow. I cannot pass up someone asking for a ride but the fact that he's standing alone far out in this barren flatness is spooky and yes, it is a man, his arm out to one side, thumb out and I stop twenty yards from him but he doesn't wave, doesn't move. Just stands there.

And then it dawns on me that it's some kind of scarecrow, somebody's idea of a joke, and I pull closer. It's a figure clothed in an old haz-mat suit, and the face is a pug face, the nose the pig-like snout of the respirator and the eyes are holes where the lenses of the mask used to be. It's a dusty silvery color, the suit cracked by the sun and wind, and one hand holds a yellow fly swatter, the other has a stub of a branch that looks like the hitchhiking thumb. A Bud Light cap is askew on its head. It's a grim thing, and now the rain starts, slanting in.

Alexander von Humboldt never set foot in Nevada. He never saw the Humboldt River or the Humboldt Range and he never touched the tiny Humboldt cutthroat trout. In fact, the only time von Humboldt came to America was in 1804, when he visited Thomas Jefferson in Washington. Von Humboldt had come from South America where he had mapped the 1,700 mile length of the Orinoco River, had climbed in the Andes to what Europeans then thought to be the highest point on earth, and had mapped the currents of the Pacific Ocean. He had found the southern magnetic pole. Jefferson persuaded him to stay long enough to help sort out what his Louisiana Purchase contained.

When he was seventy-six, the first volume of his greatest work was published. He called it *Kosmos*. Darwin said about him, "He was the greatest scientific traveler who ever lived." Von Humboldt was the first to write about the integration of humans and the earth: "Where man steps," he wrote, "his footprint changes the course of rivers, the lives of animals, the call of birds."

Children in Venezuela memorize the words of Alejandro de Humboldt who "named all the flowers and stones."

There is a Humboldt County in Kansas, another in Iowa and a third on the north coast of California. The icy current that sweeps the west coast of the Americas is called the Humboldt Current. But he was never there. Wells, Nevada, where I slept last night, nestled among a hundred eighteen wheelers was, at one time, called Humboldt Wells.

I walk off some distance from the truck until it is only a blot on the landscape and my strange ghost figure stands near it. Von Humboldt wrote, " a deep calm reigned in these solitary places." Except for the grim scarecrow and my Ford truck, it could be 1804, the year Thomas Jefferson bought Louisiana from King Louis. The French royal checkbook was empty and the king sold a chunk of real estate that stretched from New Orleans to Montana. Forty years later, Mexico ceded another empty land to the U.S. The Seven Cities of Gold had turned into rattlesnakes and sagebrush. Thunder rattles over the Snake Mountains and there is lightning above the Jarbridge Wilderness. Somewhere far in front of me is the Marys River. I wonder if it is named after the Virgin Mary or after the wife of some early settler who found a home in this solitary place.

It was, I found out later, named after explorer Peter Ogden's Indian wife. Ogden was the first white man to find this desolate opening to the west.

WILDCAT CREEK. At thirty-eight miles, the road made a sharp turn and a dip toward the west. On the map there should be a turn-off to the Gibbs ranch and sure enough, there was a big gate, a large sign that announced NO TRESPASSING. James Prosek told me to cross the next cattle guard, park, and hike west to find Wildcat Creek. It was where he had caught a Humboldt cutthroat trout. The road dips and crosses a small creek. To the west was a marshy area, cordoned off by a new fence. I parked the truck where the road rose again and set up my rod. Walk a mile or two through the sagebrush, he wrote.

So I set out. The sky was dark and occasionally rain misted. I could see the ranch buildings a mile or so south of me. Eventually I came to a clearing where there was an empty ten-wide and a corral for loading cattle. A dirt road went off to the north, but there was no sign of anyone, no tire tracks, and weeds grew around the trailer. It was obviously a seasonal dwelling where someone lived when there were cattle.

The Bull Run Mountains were far in front of me and now I could see a dark line of green a half mile off. As I came closer, I could see that it was willows. The going wasn't easy, sagebrush waist high, sometimes chest high, and there was no way I could walk in a straight line. I fought my way through the brush and now the rain suddenly came with a rattle of thunder. It lasted only a few minutes, then turned into a cold wind that numbed my hands and ears.

I came to the wall of willows and it was a nearly impenetrable tangle. There had to be water on the other side of this and I attacked, bending branches and stepping on them, back-tracking, finding my way into a small clearing only to find I was trapped, had to retreat. Sometimes I put my rod against the willows so that I could use both hands to pull them apart. Mosquitoes swarmed and suddenly there it was, the green water silently rushing between the willows.

But it was too full, swollen by the rain, and the edges were slick with mud. Cattle had degraded this creek, wading in and out of it, breaking down the banks until silt spread along the banks, soft and thick. Deer tracks were mixed with those of cattle and when I stepped into it, my boots sank to the ankles.

It took twenty minutes to thread a nymph onto my leader and I cursed my failing eyes. Somewhere I had a baseball cap with a magnifier that flipped down only I hadn't been able to find it and now I was paying the price.

The current sucked the nymph under and the leader was almost immediately taut. I tried again but I knew there was little chance of finding a trout in water surging brown like this. I couldn't wade upstream, the stream was swollen and murky and now the rain came again, slashing at the surface of the water.

I waited under the willows until it slackened, then fought my way out into the sagebrush. The smell of sage filled the air and I hiked parallel to the willows, looking for an opening where the creek might be fishable.

It was useless. I spent the next hour crashing through the tangle, trying to find a place where I could drift the nymph but it was like trying to fish in a rain-swollen drainage ditch.

Finally I gave up and set back across the sagebrush toward the truck. From a rise I could see the corral and beyond it, nearly two miles off, the dot of the truck. I worked my way through the brush, the wind rising, falling, rain again. The mountains were brindled with the shadows of the rushing clouds.

The Humboldt cutthroat trout exists in places where it's hard to imagine. The swollen stream I had found would be not much more than a trickle by mid-summer. Able to tolerate temperatures as high as 82°F, high alkalinity and incredible amounts of dissolved solids, they survive in the summer months in tiny pools. They are endangered, and the creeks, like Wildcat Creek, suffer from a century of cattle grazing. Robert Behnke, in his **Trout of America,** writes that almost all of the existing Humbolt cutts are small populations in small unstable headwater streams like Wildcat Creek, isolated from one another. It lives in "a harsh, wildly fluctuating environment of floods, droughts and the high siltation levels characteristic of arid watersheds." In other words, not where we usually look for trout.

The sagebrush was high enough so that from time to time I lost sight of the truck. There are 96 million acres of sagebrush between the Rockies and the Sierra Nevada mountains. By the time I reached the truck my hands were scarred from the sage branches and my clothes gave off the sharp smell of sage. I looked back over the sloping expanse of brush. Things lived there: snakes and ground birds and coyotes and small white-tailed deer. High above, a kestrel circled.

I ate my truck stop sandwich and started back toward Deeth. A mile later there was a pickup truck, the first sign of anyone I had seen that day. A man was working on a fence, a roll of barbed wire next to him. A dog watched me warily as I stopped. The truck belonged to a ranch hand, and when I told him I had been out on Wildcat Creek trying to catch a Humboldt cutt he said, "Too much water. Rained three days last week, mostly up higher and it won't go down for another week."

"That's the story of my life," I said. "It's always, 'you ought to have been here last week.'"

"Well," he said, "My kid caught trout out of there last week before it rained. We had them for supper."

"They're endangered, you know."

He tipped his hat back with one finger. "Sir," he said. "We're all in danger of something. You can't tell when a stranger will show up."

And here I was, a stranger in this desolate piece of landscape. Had this man put up that bizarre scarecrow? He attached the barbed wire to a pulley and stretched it tight, nailing it to the post with several staples. He did not turn when I walked back to my truck and drove off.

The dirt road seemed shorter on the return trip. I knew now where the washouts were and I made good time. I thought about the little trout in that stream. They had come there centuries ago, maybe as far back as the Pleistocene Age. Glaciers had scoured the long plain I was traversing and several thousand years ago beavers crossed over from the Lahontan basin into the Humboldt drainage. Lakes formed in their wake. Today the beaver and trout co-exist and beaver ponds on small streams allow the trout to survive harsh winters.

Behnke writes of a reservoir in the Humboldt drainage in which there is algae so thick in the summer that it resembles pea soup. The water temperature climbs into the 80's and warm water fish like crappie, sunfish and catfish have replaced the native trout. But Humboldt cutthroat trout come down into it to spawn and live there a year or two before going back upstream. "How any trout can survive and grow in such an environment is surprising," Behnke writes.

My grandsons, Nathaniel and Owen, fish for perch and bluegill in the warm backwater of a Feather River slough. There are no trout.

MARIA CALLAS. The O'Neill-Deeth county road is straight, as if someone had laid it out with a laser, and it stretches south toward the horizon. One either side are low mountains, the Snake Mountains on the east, the Jarbridge wilderness ahead and to the west. Sagebrush covers everything, olive green, and the cloud cover makes it dark, black in places. Rain splatters, drops the size of quarters splotch the windshield and the road blurs. I slow, turn on the windshield wipers and the rain stops as quickly as it started.

Something moves just off the right fender and suddenly a steer is in the road, head down, bobbing, as startled by the truck as I am startled by it and I swerve, the truck slewing to one side, barely missing it and when I stop and look back it's gone.

I take a breath, open the door and step out onto the wet road. The smell of sage fills the air. Thunder crackles somewhere, and I can see the long tendrils of the rain cloud moving north.

Maria Callas is on the disc player in the truck, and her voice rises, spiraling up and at the same moment there is movement in the sage and up come the heads of first one, then two, then another of the cattle that are invisibly grazing there. Her voice is high now, full and pulsating and the heads of the cattle are raised, turned toward the truck, as if they are an audience that has suddenly appeared. There must be more than a dozen of them, strange faces that are white and black. These cattle are all black except for the face, where white splotches are like masks, and some of them have a ghostly look, white skulls with huge black holes for the eyes and the black muzzle seems to be the empty mouth and these strange faces are turned toward her voice.

"You are my love," she sings in Italian and they are attentive, motionless, transfixed by this new voice that floats toward them. "Do not leave me."

They wait. The thunder is more distant now, a faint rumble. The wind comes up and still they look toward the truck and her voice.

They are dumb animals, I think, and they have no idea how beautiful her voice is, and if I had slammed into the steer and gone through the windshield they would have raised their heads briefly, but I would not have been their concern. Death is everywhere. It is a steer that bolts from the sagebrush and it is the electric bolt that stills a heart, as it did to my older brother. Ronald wasn't driving down a dirt road in Nevada. He was sitting at his elegant desk when the steer suddenly crossed the road, only he couldn't swerve in time.

I watch their heads as they bend to graze again and then there is nothing. They have disappeared into the brush and chaparral, leaving emptiness and the darkening sky. "I have miles to go before I sleep," Frost wrote. He was right about that.

I had come within an instant of smashing into that steer. I could imagine what would have happened: I would have slammed into it, and perhaps it would have come over the hood, smashing through the windshield. And I would have been miles from anyone who might have known what had happened to me. Miles from salvation. The seemingly endless panorama of sagebrush is not empty. If I wait, I will see grouse cross the emptiness of the road. Perhaps a coyote will suddenly appear from the brush and lope down the open graveled surface, only to disappear in the other side and the cattle continue to graze invisibly in the sage. I am an intruder. I do not belong here. It is a disquieting thought and I put the truck into gear and drive south toward Deeth.

DEETH SIDING. Great Uncle Howard and my mother commuted to San Francisco on the ferry. The Bay was black at night, no lights because the war was still on. There were seven of us at the dinner table at night, sometime as many as nine: Aunt Edna and Uncle Howard, my two brothers and I, our mother, Aunt Laura, and sometimes Eva Baer or Mr. Brown, who rented rooms in the house on Carmel Avenue. On the way home from work, Uncle Howard would strike up a conversation with a young soldier or sailor bound for the Pacific. Invariably they were from Iowa or Illinois or Kansas and by the time the ferry docked in Oakland, Aunt Edna had another person to feed. Aunt Edna kept everybody's ration book, and she was adept at trading sugar stamps for meat, a meat stamp for enough sugar to make a cake, finding ways to extend the meal when there were extra mouths at the table. She never knew when her husband would show up with another 19-year-old in a sailor uniform, shy and nervous, but there was a mid-western dinner, a meatloaf or a pot roast, lots of mashed potatoes and gravy. It must have seemed like a touch of home to them.

Paul and I slept in a room in the basement and there was an army cot along one wall. This was where the soldier or sailor would end up for the night.

The train that brought us west was filled with soldiers and sailors. When my father was told he had tuberculosis, Aunt Edna and Uncle Howard were the ones who took us in. My father went off to the magic mountain in New Mexico and my mother, my brothers and I spent three days and four nights on that train coming west from Illinois. Paul had his seventh birthday on the train. I would turn ten when we arrived in Oakland.

The porters made up the Pullman berths every night, folding the seats back, pulling down the beds, drawing the curtains. Ronald slept in an upper berth, Paul and I shared a lower. We had a window, and the night landscape rushed by, lights that came and went, far-off houses, sometimes a town. The long aisle of the car was a narrow dark corridor, the green curtains covering the berths on either side. There were the voices of people behind those curtains, women in robes who emerged to walk to the far end of the car where there was a washroom. Most of the passengers were young men bound for the Pacific war. The heavy cloth bulged and moved as people readied their beds, struggled to put clothes into the hanging nets. A curtain opened to let someone climb to an upper berth. and then, when it got late, the voices stopped. The corridor was empty. If I went down to the men's toilet at the end of the car, I would find the black porter shining shoes, and sometimes men who were smoking, standing in their uniform trousers and undershirts.

There was a cousin who was a bomber crewman in the Pacific war. I met him once. He drowned in the sea off Guam. Not because his plane went down. He was swimming. He survived air combat, numerous missions over Japan, and celebrating the end of the war, died like a tourist.

The war ended and the lights went back on in the Bay. It was filled with ships and suddenly the big sign in Emeryville was there. Coming off the Bay Bridge in the evening we were faced with SHERWIN WILLIAMS PAINT in huge letters and then a globe with the outline of North America. A can of neon paint tipped over it and red light splashed like paint and the sign flashed, COVERS THE EARTH as the red lights covered the globe.

The soldiers and sailors disappeared, the ration books stayed in the drawer in the kitchen table and we drove in Uncle Howard's 1939 Packard to the McCloud River. I caught a trout that summer.

The Pullman cars are gone. So are the great steam engines, the twenty-wheeled Malleys that made the ground shake. Standing at the siding in Deeth this afternoon, looking out across the Nevada sagebrush toward the Ruby Mountains, I can imagine that long-ago train rushing past. A family lived in the abandoned house behind me. There was a store. Paul and I might have seen the lights at night.

But Deeth, which had been formerly named *Death,* was empty. Somewhere to the north of me was a trout that should have been dead, too. But for several thousand years it had managed to adapt to the harsh conditions of the high desert, and against all odds it had survived. Survival. Some of us do, some of us don't.

CARLIN, NEVADA is twenty-three miles west of Elko. In 1951 it was bisected by a two-lane blacktop, the transcontinental "Lincoln Highway." Carlin was small and sleepy and intolerably hot on a summer day, temperature plummeting below freezing in the winter. The Humboldt River was there as well, and shallow ponds along the railroad tracks froze in the winter. The Pacific Fruit Express Company, owners of the bright yellow refrigerator cars that carried fresh produce east, owned those ponds, and the ice was sixteen inches thick. It was cut into blocks, and packed in sawdust in the long, low wooden sheds that paralleled the Southern Pacific tracks.

I arrived at midnight. I had started on the Greyhound bus at nine that morning in Oakland. My great uncle, who worked for the railroad, had gotten me a summer job at the icing station in Carlin. The railroad cars, called reefers, had big compartments at each end that were filled with ice. The first icing stop was in Roseville, the next in Carlin. Across the country, the trains stopped while men on catwalks pushed huge chucks of ice down through the hatches at either end. I remember my parents being hesitant about a sixteen year old boy going off to the high desert and I was, by no means a strapping teenager. I was skinny and what possessed my great uncle to wangle the job for me remains a mystery. Perhaps Uncle Howard remembered his own teenage years. He left school at the end of eighth grade, learned Morse Code, and became a railroad telegrapher, bouncing from railroad to railroad until the First World War. Now he was a clerk with the Pacific Fruit Express, rode the ferry to San Francisco each morning and walked to New Montgomery Street where he kept track of the yellow cars carrying California fruit across the country. I suppose he thought that at sixteen I ought to be striking out on my own, too.

There I was, at midnight, the Nevada landscape black as pitch, few lights in the tiny town, and I stumbled into a bar, asked where the icing station was, and was told which cross street would lead me to the tracks. I spent the night in a bunk in a dormitory, surrounded by snoring men and the smell of sweat. At some point in the early hours a bell rang and the men climbed out of beds, pulled on work boots and gloves and heavy shirts and went out into the night.

The next morning I saw where they had gone. Sheet metal catwalks paralleled the tracks, jutting out far enough so that blocks of ice skidded along the metal surface could be tipped over into waiting cars. Two men worked each end of a car, one pulling the blocks of ice to the edge, the other using a long pike pole with a steel tip to shove them into the open hatch.

To the south were the Cortez Mountains, to the east was the Ruby Range, and as far as I could see, a lumpy landscape of sagebrush stretched away, already shimmering in the heat. I found the foreman and explained who I was and he looked at me doubtfully.

"You don't look eighteen," he said.

"I'm not," I showed him the letter that offered me the job.

"Shit," he said. "You ever do anything like this?"

He showed me the ice hook that I would carry, asked if I had gloves.

"No," I said. "Nobody said to bring gloves."

"Shit," he said again. He found leather gloves for me, with thick cracked fingers and he said, "Reefers come though at different times. No schedule, so we roust you out when there's a train to ice. You get up there." He pointed to the catwalk. "First thing you do is shine a light down into the hatch, make sure there's no hobo down there out of the wind. Mostly they know better, but every once in a while there's some dumb son of a bitch in there, and one a these blocks weighs three hundred pounds. Your job is to pull the ice over to the loader. He pushes them into the hatch. They come up there." He pointed to a motionless conveyor belt that rose from a loading platform to the catwalk.

The ice, packed in sawdust in the ice house, was sixteen inches thick, a foot and a half wide and three feet long.

"You ain't gonna last long," he said. He was right.

That afternoon I worked my first train. The men were a rough mix: Greek and Irish and Canadians and roustabouts from Oregon and Washington, in their thirties or forties, working for not much more than minimum wage, ninety cents an hour, nine dollars for a ten hour shift. Part of the shift was spent lying in a hot bunk or smoking in the ice house that smelled of wet sawdust and was a welcome relief from the Nevada midday heat. When the train came in we mounted the metal catwalk and a truck appeared below, loaded with blocks of ice. The ice came up onto the metal surface, skidding in the heat, and I drove my ice hook into a block, tugging it toward the man who waited with the pike pole. Other men slid the blocks easily across the hot surface, but I struggled, trying not to get overrun by three hundred pounds of ice

"Come on, kid," my partner called. "We ain't got all day." I tried not to slip, not wearing boots like the other men, wearing tennis shoes and struggling to muscle the ice toward him.

"Fuckin' A, get a move on," he yelled, and it was the first time I heard the word "fucking" yelled at me. A switch engine pushed the cars under the catwalk, three cars loaded at a time, and I managed to keep up, but only barely. By the time the nearly one hundred cars were loaded with ice, I was exhausted. I had not slipped off the catwalk. I had not been crushed by a sliding block of ice, but I knew that there was no way I could last a summer doing this work. The sagebrush shimmered in the heat, willowy waves rising from it, and the mountains shivered, grey nebulous images that hovered above the horizon. And I knew that I would get on a bus that evening and go back to California and the house in Berkeley and for the rest of the summer I would bag groceries for rich Berkeley women and carry their bags to their cars and my great uncle would be disappointed in me.

I was not what he had been. At my age he had gone off to boom around the country, tapping his telegraph key, living in rooming houses in the mining towns of Colorado and Nevada and throughout the West, standing on the edge of tracks in the night, holding up a ring with a message for the engineer of a passing train, his face only inches from the pounding driving wheels that roared past.

When the shift was over I told the foreman I was leaving. He said nothing.

I walked back into town, had a sandwich at a café and waited. The bus came in the early evening. The blue greyhound on the side was dust-covered, and I settled into the seat, my body aching. I dozed most of the trip, waking when the bus stopped in Reno, waking again when it labored up the impossible switchbacks of Donner Summit.

I arrived in Oakland late the next morning.

My parents said nothing.

I had gone off and I had returned. I offered no explanation.

NAMES ON THE LAND. The moon is still up. This is the long-night moon, the full moon that comes in December and the road to the top of the ridge is pale blue. At two this morning, Mars was next to the moon. I know that only because a woman on the radio explained how Mars had turned its full face toward the sun and was at its brightest. I stood in the bathroom and looked up through the glass above the shower at the moon and the brilliant light next to it. I could not sleep and I thought of Achilles on the beach at Troy, how the torch bearers came between the upturned hulls of the ships with his lover's body and above them might have been this same moon and Mars, too.

Coming down from the ridge this morning there was no sound. No dog bark. No rooster. There was a sighing in the trees at the far end of the meadow. I listened for the car of the newspaper man. Last night Ethan Newby and I talked about fishing in the summer. I will go to Nevada and find the Humboldt cutthroat trout, I said, and later I went out onto the deck and looked at the outline of the mountain and remembered.

The high desert in the northeastern corner of Nevada is bordered on one side by the Snake Range. To the west of those mountains, the Marys River drainage runs south from Oregon toward the Humboldt River. There are dozens of creeks. The names fascinate me. Who was Susie, or Maggie? Were they wives or sweethearts or daughters? Was Pete Hansen a friend or a brother of the first person to find the creek, or did Pete Hansen name the creek after himself? Maybe he died there. Toe Jam Creek and Pie Creek. Four creeks are named First Boulder Creek, Second Boulder, Third Boulder and Fourth Boulder. Landmarks to find where you were in a land where the sagebrush stretches for miles and after an hour of driving on a dirt road, so straight it looks as if it were laid out with a laser beam, a plume of dust behind the truck, the road still disappears into the distance. And then I cross T Creek, and wonder why it's marked that way on the map. Someone's initial? A sudden branching of the creek? Was it the color of tea after a passing thundershower and the map maker wrote just the letter and not the word? Sheep Creek and Secret Creek and Winters Creek and Box Canyon and Rattlesnake. There is a Crane Canyon Creek where someone must have seen cranes. Of course, there's a Trout Creek. And a Cottonwood. Someone named Conners has a creek named after him or his family. Perhaps there was a ranch there at one time. Now there is only the pale green expanse of sagebrush There is a Nelson Creek, too, just as there is a Nelson Creek that empties into California's Feather River, but this one isn't in a deep canyon in the shade of firs and pines.

There are birds: Ground Dove and Rock Wren and Water Pipit and Rosy Finch. The Water Pipit is rarely seen because it's a ground bird, scurrying beneath the sagebrush. It seems strange for a bird whose name contains the word *water*, to live in this arid landscape, but there are marshes fifty miles south along the Humboldt River. The Ground Dove, like its name, and the Rock Wren are terrestrial birds, too. They can, of course, fly, but they prefer to keep hidden from the hawks that circle high above.

Near Deeth there is a marsh and there was an egret, solitary, like a white exclamation mark in the dark green. I have a fondness for egrets. They appear in the rice fields off highway 162 in the Sacramento Valley, stalking crawdads. They lift off from the trees along the Feather River, their long wings rowing against the upriver wind.

This egret was among marsh grasses that marked a sink in a creek that was aimed at the Humboldt River. But the creek settled into the ground, and there was no outlet, only the olive sagebrush that bordered the Southern Pacific tracks.

DAYBREAK. FIRST LIGHT. Wells, Nevada. A 22-wheeler double trailer crawls out of the Flying J truck stop, headlights on, a Christmas tree of orange and red lights. The driver shifts up through the gears, the truck laboring, gaining speed for the interstate. A rooster crows. A dog barks.

The gray sagebrush, stretches toward the Ruby Mountains. The sun touches the peaks, lighting the ridges. Cattle are darker lumps among the sage. Some of the eighteen wheelers rocketing along have their headlights off.

In Reno the city lights rise against the dark eastern slope of the Sierras. A motel sign blinks 39.95. A woman with a paper cup full of quarters pulls the handle of a slot machine in the half-empty casino. There are no clocks.

The night spotlights at the inspection station on the highway switch off

The sun slides off the shoulder of Mt. Lassen. Steam rises from Lake Almanor. A solitary boat drifts in the gray, the fisherman indistinct. A trout rises at the edge near the reeds. Water laps in the shadow of the pines.

In the Humbug Valley, trees are dark columns against the gray sky. Across the meadow, mist rises leaving a long white ribbon at the black base of the forest. Birdsong drifts. The creek chuckles.

In Chico a small boy pads barefoot down the hallway to the bathroom. He stands at the toilet, half-awake, pees and then goes into the living room,. The old dog sits at the sliding glass door. The boy climbs onto the couch, curls up, drawing his knees to his chest and goes back to sleep. The dog watches as the sun filters through the maple. A cat drops off the fence, picks its way warily into the yard,. The dog watches it intently.

Along the coast the houses are still dark. A cop waits in a small town, parked on the empty main street. His shift is almost over. It will be light when he goes home to his sleeping family.

III
The Dark Current

THE RIVER. I drove up the Central Valley last night to my oldest son's house and the next morning we rose in the darkness to go fishing for steelhead on the Feather River. I was awake long before I heard his voice at the bedroom door. This last year I've been awake at strange hours, lying in bed in the blackness looking at the ceiling at two or three in the morning, sometimes rising, and going out to the family room where I turn on the television and watch old movies or go through old boxes of photographs. Occasionally I take a flashlight and go for a walk on the dark streets, walk until the sky begins to grow light. Perhaps it's a function of old age. All I know is that I don't sleep much any more.

Geoffrey called through the door, "Dad, you up?" and I rose and put my clothes on and I went out into the kitchen where he had eggs and coffee ready. The house was quiet, his children and his wife asleep, the dog dozing in front of the sliding glass door that looked out onto the black back yard.

We drove for an hour until we came to the turn-off, leaving the pavement for a rutted dirt road that led out through a maze of levees and sloughs, the road looking worse in the headlights than it was. Once he shifted into four-wheel drive as we dropped down a steep slope, rising again onto the main levee where the road leveled out, becoming smooth gravel.

There was a sharp wind. We parked on the top of the levee with the river below, a presence, wide, flat, a lightness in the dark, water rushing, sliding over rocks, and we rigged our rods by flashlight. I pulled on a sweater over the chest waders, my fishing vest, a coat, flaps over ears, fingerless gloves, wrapped against the November cold.

We finished the last of the coffee, waited until the sky started to lighten, the river becoming faint, rocks taking shape, then started down the levee on foot. An owl called. Earlier, on the road we were startled when an owl flashed suddenly onto the windshield, white wings spread almost as wide as the glass before slipping up over the top of the cab.

When I waded into the river I could feel the current take hold, wrapping itself around my calves, and I braced myself with the wading staff, went out thirty feet to where the wide riffle shelved off into deeper water. The cast was easy with the wind at my back, but the fly dragged immediately, swung down into the current, and I retrieved it under water, as if it were a nymph. Ahead of me violet-green swallows darted, slicing low on the water, suddenly holding with a flutter of wings to take an insect, drop a wing and scoot back in the opposite direction. They worked back and forth among each other, a wondrous looping with long arrow-like flights only inches from the surface. Overhead an osprey wheeled, and downstream there were pelicans, lined up on a log, white statues waiting for the shad to arrive.

The sky was piling up darker to the west over the Central Valley and the rain dotted the surface around me, the wind so cold that my hands were like ice. What looked like a little old man, hunched over on the point upstream was a great blue heron, motionless, waiting, and, watching him, I was unprepared for the sudden slam on the end of the line as a steelhead took the fly and immediately broke it off. Shit! I tied another one on, my frozen fingers slow to obey. A few casts later and another fish broke off another fly. Now the rain came sideways, the water gray-green and moving continuously so that, unless I paid attention, I began to feel as if I were moving, my feet planted on the bottom, but the water motionless and my body sliding upstream. The heron lifted off the point, his huge wings unfolding and folding as he rowed slowly toward the valley. I waded out a bit farther until the current gripped at me and I turned and watched Geoff's figure upstream, working his way across.

The river is gray and the current surges, sucking at my legs and I am unsure of my footing, watch the surface shift and slide in the half-light, and I back out, stumbling on the rocks. For the first time in my life I am afraid of the river.

When I was fourteen I remember going to the Friday night football game at Piedmont High School, under the lights in the tiny stadium at the foot of the hill and then climbing back up to Piedmont Avenue and the social hall in the church where there was a dance and standing along the side of the semi-dark room, watching girls I wanted to dance with, afraid to step out into the current of dancers, much the same way I am afraid to step out into the current of the river this morning. I didn't know then what I was afraid of. Girls danced with other girls while boys stood, transfixed, palms sweaty, perhaps afraid that we would appear to be clumsy or foolish and I waited, the time falling toward the last dance and then I went out into the night where the last streetcar rattled along the avenue, nearly empty, light spilling out onto the now wet pavement.

Now, facing the river, I am afraid to step into it, afraid to dance with the dark current.

The light grew at the window. What had been a black

square in the wall was now grey. Beyond the window was the river and I could hear the faint rush through the wall. As I watched, the window grew lighter, dim outlines of the trees on the opposite side of the canyon coming into focus.

I remembered waking as a teenager in the tent cabin in the summer camp where I worked. There were ordinarily four beds on each platform, white canvas covers hung over the wooden frame. The fabric was aged grey, the sides roped up and there were only two occupants in that tent, myself and Doug, the camp lifeguard. I lay on my side and watched trees and rocks take shape as it grew light. How long ago was that? And would anyone else remember it? Did someone else from that summer lie awake this morning and look at a window and think about a morning more than a half century past?

The tent platform faded, replaced by the semi-dark room. Now the pines on the opposite side of the canyon were clear. But the slope next to the tent platform lingered. Beyond was the indistinct road that wound through the camp. I would have to get up, pull on my pants and shirt and boots, go to the dining hall where I stood in the back, next to the huge walk-in refrigerator and smoked a cigarette, the warmth of the kitchen coming through the screen doors.

When the memory disappears, so do we. Or perhaps it's the other way around. From the Latin, *vice versa,* to take the opposite position. You're here. You're not here. You were eighteen, lying on your bed looking at a blue jay in the early morning light and then you were not eighteen. The tent platform has disappeared and Doug, too, is gone, an aneurysm bursting in his head when he was sixty.

There are few left who remember those tents or those mornings. It remains a secret, a word almost unchanged since its Latin origin from *secretus:* withdrawn, hidden, kept private. A story that I hold inside, perhaps shared with someone I trust to keep from others. Not to be left lying on the desk or folded in a pocket of the suit that is brought to the funeral parlor. Not that this memory is important, or that its broadcast would reveal inner thoughts that I want no one else to know. But it is a part of me, part of my fabric, just as the rush of the unseen river is part of my fabric

Was it the same river, or was it a different one where egrets lifted off from the trees and rowed downstream or the river that rushed over stones or a river that meandered slowly, while the drift boat turned to face the dark water? Was it the river with pocket water where I waded, waist deep, casting into the next pool, or the river where my youngest son waded up to his chest, making a long effortless cast into water shaded by pines seventy feet away? Was it the river in November when I sat beneath the trees and watched the rain turn to snow, the flakes dissolving as they touched the water?

I rose from the bed, padded into the kitchen, put water into a pan on the stove, turned the flame on and spooned coffee into a filter. I waited for the water to boil, listening to the faint rush of the river, remembering the water ouzel that had slipped off the rock in front of me, dropping into the clear water to work its way against the current. John Muir's dipper.

IT IS ALMOST WINTER. Mist smokes through the pines and below us wild-eyed steelhead fin in the dark water. We float unconscious of them, and their urge to find the exact spot where they were conceived; they wait for the rain to bring sediment, cloud the river, and we bump over the rocks, the guide rows hard, his back knotted, swinging the boat away from the rock face and now rain dimples the water, turns the green to black, always the rush of water, the white noise that fills the November air.

We pass named pools, Crash and Burn where an old automobile body hangs high on the canyon wall, Barbie where a Barbie doll was nailed to a tree. The Culvert, an empty concrete box and The Dead Mexican.

Was it a body that washed onto those rocks? Did he meet his death on the curve in the highway far above? The indicator dips and the guide barks at us to strip line but there is no fish. They are silver-sided muscles with a tiny brain that connects them to their journey. The rain is harder, slanting sideways. These fish come up to the very point where they were conceived.

I do not know where I was conceived. Somewhere in Illinois where snow falls and fields turn white. Cows cluster around hay bales dropped from a truck. They do not give birth in the same field where they were born. There is no river noise on the prairie. Only the wind and the summer thunder and in the winter the snow swallows all sound.

Soon this rain will turn to snow, put white caps on the rocks, mute the river, drift through the pines, and it will be the Dead of Winter. Spent salmon drift up on the rocks; crows and ravens pick at them. The boat slips through a long run, silent. Beneath us the steelhead wait.

I WAS TOLD THAT EDWARD BLACKBEARD TEACH harbored his ship in Turneffe Atoll in 1718, just off the coast of what was to become British Honduras, now Belize. I remembered the description of Teach from *Howard Pyle's Book of Pirates*, vivid color plates that showed bearded men with swords, ships on fire in the Caribbean night, a gathering of men burying trunks of treasure. As a boy, I devoured those stories. I remembered Lieutenant Robert Maynard hunting down Teach in the Carolinas and nailing his head to the bowsprit of his ship before sailing home to England.

I fished in Turneffe Atoll with Geoffrey, Graham and Ethan Newby on my seventieth birthday. Birds shrieked from the tangled mangroves, cries like car alarms and rusty chains being dragged across tin roofs. Barracuda with jagged teeth, their bodies half head and mouth struck at Graham's bait and bent the hook, running a hundred yards before leaping into the air. Silver torpedoes of bonefish snatched my fly and ran, bending the rod double. At evening I stood on the edge of the grass and looked toward the reef where the breakers thundered. Wind came up, bending the palms and mangroves. Clouds of mosquitoes swarmed. I tried to imagine Teach and his crew among the mangroves, waiting for some passing Spanish ship. But Teach wasn't particular about whom he captured, and Maynard was the one who tracked him down. In my journal of that week at Turneffe, I wrote:

Today I took three bonefish. Graham caught four. One was a three and a half pounder. We walked the turquoise flats for an hour, circling a single mangrove island that rose out of the water, the long line of the surf behind it. A school of bones next to the island suddenly erupted in an explosion on the surface.

"'Cuda!" said our guide, Dubs. "He launch from there." He pointed behind us. "I see him going to get something to eat." A barracuda had driven past us into the school in search of something to prey on.

The school of fish shot north into deeper water, a dark cloud pushing the surface in a surge, and it exploded again.

That evening as I watched the Caribbean darken, I thought of how Blackbeard Teach had waited for his prey. Like the barracuda, he had waited for the right moment, then pounced. His ship, the Queen Anne's Revenge, was a French merchant ship that he captured and fitted with forty guns.

He captured a ten-gun sloop, Adventure, in 1718 at Turneffe, forcing its captain to join him. Edward Robinson, the ship's gunner was later involved in the Battle of Cape Fear River, and Israel Hands was made captain of the captured ship. They sailed for North Carolina, where Teach eventually met his end. The local legend was that Blackbeard's headless body remained in the Caribbean, haunting its waters.

MIDMORNING at the San Francisco casting ponds. There is a man working out line with a spey rod, long figure-eight loops. I am at the west side, and there is no wind, only bright sun at our backs. My rod is older than me, bamboo, something from another time. It was given to me by Wayne Morris who, when he turned one hundred, gave me his rod with the admonition that I should fish with it, not let it become something to hang on the wall.

I raise the line from the water and the back cast is flat, and I drive the rod forward and pump the line with my left hand and suddenly the double-haul works! The line surges and floats in the air, gossamer, Norman Maclean said, and there is a beauty in what I have done. I remember the Big Blackfoot, wide riffles only knee deep and dark trees on the far side, a long cast and that double haul and the fly in the shadow of the pines and the sudden explosion in the water. I cast again, pump the line once more and it is like a prayer, answered. Both powerful and delicate. Quite beautiful.

Graham is almost chest-deep in Montana's Blackfoot. He is casting to the darkness on the far side of the river and Geoff and I watch as the line snakes out, is suspended in the air, slips back until it is fully extended behind, him, only a few feet above the surface and then, with a powerful stroke it moves into the dark green of the forest shadow.

"He's so fucking good,' I say to Geoffrey.

"Yes, he is."

But if we say it to Graham he looks puzzled, as if everyone can do what he does. When he was eight I watched him on the street in front of the house. In our family you had to be ten to go off fishing. I learned that from Art, who said they had to be old enough to be successful. "Any younger and they get frustrated, and they quit," he had said. It happened that way with his own son.

So Geoffrey was ten when he went onto the Little Truckee and the Middle Fork of the Feather with me and his uncle and he caught trout and Art was right. But Graham was impatient. And there he was in the street, laying out enough line so that I could not refuse him. And now, chest deep in the Blackfoot, he is a poem with a four-count rhythm.

RAIN ON THE ROOF, tapping and then thudding, rain on the porch when I open the door, rain on my head and shoulders, rain on the river. I sit under the trees and watch it dimple the river, rain so heavy it forces me to pull over to the side of the road; rain in Shillingstone, a steady even rain, not heavy, a rain that saturates. I ride home on the bicycle in the rain, lorries splashing me as they pass. Mrs. Goddard's cows stand head down in the rain, motionless. Rain in the mountains, drumming on the tin roof of the cabin, sheeting off in a curtain at the edge of the roof. The gas fire in the wall bubbles. Rain on the street, the pavement slick and black, reflecting the streetlight on the corner. Rain in Iowa City, a sudden pounding rain as the storm passes over, thunder rumbling, lightning suddenly illuminating the room. Rain on a hot Florida afternoon, and when it stops, a skin of tiny green frogs covers the window of the café. Rain far off, a thin grey sheet descending on the high desert north of Ely. Rain on the skylight as I write this, like fingernails tapping on a table, an impatient person waiting for an answer.

THE SIERRA SKY LODGE, made of six by six pecky cedar, laid like logs, warm in the winter, too warm in the summer. Opposite is highway 70, the whine of logging trucks before dawn, the road rain slick in October.

Layman's Resort, tiny cabins sided with the bark scabs cut from logs at the mill, usually discarded or dropped into the burner. Names like Trout and Squirrel, two cabins I have stayed in. Art Morris and I stayed in Trout cabin, drank a cold beer on the tiny porch, fished the Middle Fork above the bridge, had dinner at Mt. Tomba. At night in Squirrel the low rush of the river fills the air. In the afternoon a hamburger BBQed over a grill, at night a low moon over the pines, a bathroom scabbed onto the north side, with a lean-to roof.

High rise in San Francisco, a view of Nob Hill, endless white sheets and white pillows.

The Gold Pan Motel in Quincy, like every other motel in the country, the same painting on velvet screwed to the wall, same thin towels.

A Patel motel in Stockton, polyester sheets after a white meal in the diner next door, a dinner with white bread, white turkey meat, white gravy, white rice.

Jim Crow cabin on the North Fork of the Yuba, a deck overlooking the creek, a tiny gas fireplace, long steps down to the cabin.

Roaches in a late night stop somewhere in Wyoming, scattering when the light was turned on.

Mosquitoes in a motel in King City, hot summer night, endless whining. When I complained, asked for a room with screens, the desk clerk gave me a can of Raid, This ought to do the trick, he said. I left before dawn, driving John's VW bug to Santa Monica.

Herrington's Resort in Sierra City, a long motel-like building with a deck for each room facing the river and a thin silver waterfall on the opposite side of the canyon. Sit on that deck with a gin and ice in the late afternoon.

The rooms at Tobin in the Canyon, a trout pond with a knot of trout; somewhere in the center was a trout that had a bend in its body as if it had been caught in a door. A long bar that was crowded when the highway was under construction but now was usually empty.

The bar halfway up the Canyon where the piano player belted out Fats Waller tunes, three fingers on one hand, two on the other, the result of a logging accident. If you closed your eyes and listened, he had all ten fingers.

The Truckee Hotel with earplugs next to the bed. Big diesel locomotives rumbled nearby most of the night, waiting for the green light to go over Donner Summit. The ear plugs did not dampen the vibration of the room.

The motel in Yuba City where I spent the night after I dumped Art's ashes in Nelson Creek. I do not remember that motel, only that the next morning when I drove down through the Valley there were snow geese on every field.

THERE ARE THIRTY-ONE railroad tunnels in the Feather River Canyon. Years ago, when the giant Malley steam locomotives came up the canyon, you could hear them almost an hour before they arrived. Suddenly the noise ceased, only to reappear a few seconds later, louder. The engine had gone into one of those tunnels. There was a long tunnel below Oakland Camp and it was necessary to walk through it to fish Spanish Creek below that point. The tunnel had a bend, so that when I was in the middle, the openings on either end disappeared and it was so black that I had to blow on my hand to know that it was in front of my face. It was a long tunnel, and the fear was that I might get caught in that tunnel when a train entered. The passenger train, the Zephyr, came down canyon in the mid-morning, up canyon in the midafternoon, but freight trains were unscheduled and there was always the apprehension that one of them would suddenly fill the tunnel, leaving no time to escape. Once that happened to me. The tunnel resounded with the roar of the engine, the brilliant light on the front revolved, catching the walls, the tracks, and me; the engineer pulled the horn and it was ear-splitting. I did as I had been told by Charlie Way, the caretaker at camp, turning to the tunnel wall, pressing my body and face against the concrete wall, waiting out the train. A hundred freight cars rattled past, only a few feet from my body, the rush of wind was constant, and then, mercifully, the last car passed and the silence in the tunnel was deafening. What had that engineer imagined when my shape appeared in the blackness? Surely he would have seen my fly rod and he must have known what I was doing.

I remembered words from my wife's brother, who was an engineer for the Illinois Central. Wendell, drove the Metro commuter trains south from Chicago and he had lost count of the number of people who had stumbled into the path of his engine. Some of them had been accidental, but others had chosen that moment to commit suicide. When I asked Wendell how he felt, he said he was pissed off. He was angry that they had thought the engine ran itself and there wasn't a human being in charge. They had chosen him to end their lives.

The Budd Car, a single diesel-powered unit that had seats

and a baggage compartment, an engineer in the front, much like a streetcar, ran down the canyon past Oakland Camp in the evening. Four of us, two boys and two girls, flagged it down. We rode as far as Belden, got off and crossed the bridge to the tiny bar that was next to the highway. There, we drank beer and played the jukebox and danced and then, in the small hours, walked back to Belden, waited for the up-canyon Budd Car on its way to Salt Lake City, flagged it down, and rode the hour to camp. One of us stayed awake to remind the conductor to stop. We passed through that last tunnel and got off in a quiet camp. We went to the path that led to the girls' tents and we grappled with each other and kissed and wandered off to our beds and sometime in the night another freight train rumbled through the cut above the camp, but we barely heard it. Now, I have heard the long complaining sound of the horn as it approached Camp Layman on the Middle Fork, a sound in the night that reawakened those memories. It passed, and there was that familiar silence.

DOGS AND CHILDREN and the dark green water under the willows. Gossamer winged mayflies around a bulb that hangs over the gate next to the stock tank. Cicadas begin their metallic chorus, a steady rasp that will last until dawn.

The armored shells of stonefly nymphs, the hollow exoskeletons cling to rocks after the stonefly nymph emerges as an adult. They live relatively short lives, sometimes as little as ninety seconds before dropping eggs on the rocks or the water. Trout rise in vicious strikes at stoneflies as they hatch, catching them in their most vulnerable moment.

Is time speeded up for the stonefly? If a dog ages seven years for every year a human lives, is the ninety seconds of a stonefly's life equivalent to my eighty-three years? I see fifteen year old dogs that look and act the way I do, taking small steps, grey on their muzzles, no longer barking at birds and cars, content to lie and wait for the person who tied their leash to the bicycle rack. Is that the path for stoneflies? Do they go through their teenage years in a matter of seconds, arriving as child-bearing adults in less time than it takes to make a free throw? A friend had a turtle. Appropriately named Mister Turtle, he moved slowly toward the lettuce that was set out for him, taking tiny crescent shaped bites. Mister Turtle lived a long time. A stonefly was not much more than a fraction of a second for Mister Turtle. Apparently turtles' hearts are less complicated than ours. According to one heart surgeon, the human heart is made to work well for almost forty years, but as life expectancy has increased, the human heart has adapted, now beating steadily for, in my case, more than eighty years. Researchers reported in Nature magazine that the heart and brain would not cease working until a hundred and fifteen years, assuming nothing else went wrong. Either way, Mr.Turtle had us beat. The turtle's heart beats more slowly, hence its long life. Insects have an open circulatory system, and a vessel along one side opens and closes, pumping the fluid that is akin to our blood.

Once we stopped at an old stone-walled motel in Arizona on a hot summer night. Heat lightning played in the mountains to the north, and thunder was a long time arriving. Insects were attracted to a light bulb at the side of the motel. Big toads gathered at the perimeter of the circle of light on the ground, and as mayflies and moths came too close to the hot bulb and suddenly fell, the toads gobbled them up. I watched for a while and then went to the hot room where an old swamp cooler tried vainly to cool things off. Geoffrey's dog and I slept fitfully. A cricket was somewhere in the room. If I rose to find it, it stopped. It was a slender green thing somewhere in that room, trying to find a mate. Not here, I thought.

AUDUBON. It's July and the hex hatch on Lake Almanor is late this year. A long, wet spring and a heavy snow pack has meant that creeks and rivers were full at the end of June and everything, wildflowers and insect hatches, is late. There are four of us, a young couple, Ellen and Chris Strempek, I have taught to fly fish, and my son, Geoffrey. I have two tubes and Geoff has brought an extra float tube up from Chico and we set them up in the late afternoon. By the time we push off from shore, the sun is low over the trees at the western edge of the lake. There is one other float tuber not far from us, and far out of the cove a couple of boats troll slowly. The lake is calm, the water flat and dark. A pair of grebes comes out from the reeds along the shore and we cast, turning slowly in circles. Geoff moves off toward the far side of the cove. Now the hatch begins. The sun has dropped behind the trees and the cove is dark. On the far side of the lake there is still light on the mountains, but a fire north of Chester has left smoke in the air and they are pink and orange.

Hatching Mayflies struggle in the surface tension of the water and the rise begins, soft sucking noises followed by a widening ring in the water as trout come up to pick off the insects. The insects use the surface tension of the water to shuck their wing cases, then struggle for a few seconds longer, unfolding their wings before they can become airborne. And in those few seconds they are vulnerable. W.C.Stewart wrote in The Practical Angler in 1857, "the May-fly is the most killing when the waters are large and dark-coloured, and then must be used close to the edges."

The insects are breaking the surface like popcorn. Bats are out, suddenly dozens of them skimming the surface of the lake like giant insects and there is a family of grebes. When I cast, the fly sits on the surface and one of the grebes turns toward it. I pull it off, cast in another direction to a rising trout. Geoff is a black blot now, and I hear him whoop and something splashes near him and I know he has a sizeable trout on.

The trees are black, the lake is a gun metal sheet stretching east to the far shore, the mountains outlined against the growing night sky. Bats slip erratically past my head and I'm casting blind, waiting for something to hit the fly, listening, holding the rod tip up, leaning forward and although the hatch continues, the trout no longer rise. One comes up near the shore, leaving a black swirl in the water. We head in, coming slowly together, voices calling out as we kick our way to the shallow incline where we launched.

I am stiff when I finally put my feet on the bottom, stagger a bit, trying to hold my balance, and walk backward as I drag the tube out of the water, trying not to stumble on my frog feet. I am reminded of part of a Yeats poem:

I will arise and go now, for always night and day
I hear lake water lapping with low sounds by the shore
. . . I hear it in the deep heart's core.

The far shore of the lake is vague, but the outline of the mountains is sharp, the sky a dark blue. There is an Audubon painting in which a blue heron is in the foreground and behind it is the shore of a river, dark and almost indistinguishable. Audubon had a teenaged boy who painted riverbanks for him. The original paintings were not like the ones we see in books. They had pieces of birds cut out and pasted onto the sheet so that some paintings were literally collages. There were lightly penciled instructions to the lithographers, and he hired out his riverbanks. I think of that teenaged boy, accompanying Audubon down a forgotten river, egrets and herons lifting off, perhaps a loon crying out, the drone of mosquitoes and the smell of mud and dank vegetation, sketching the banks and the shadowy trees and filling in the colors, so many greens, blues, browns, darkening forests and riverbanks behind the birds.

I think of Dave as a teenaged boy, riding his motorcycle, and now behind their boat as Laurel guns the engine, rising on his water skis. Or casting into the surf at Dillon Beach waiting for the surf perch to strike. Diving for abalone on the North coast, rising from the water in his wet suit.

BIRDS. Take away their feathers and their bodies are tiny, the skulls miniature, all eyes and beak.

The bluebird wears a blue cap and cape and the sand hill crane wears a red cap. The red-winged blackbird has red and yellow epaulets on its shoulders and the Stellar jay has a blue crown, like a warrior's tufted helmet. The water ouzel is soft grey, and shy. The merganser is sharp-beaked with a russet crest and flies astoundingly fast. In the pre-dawn darkness an owl suddenly materialized at the windshield of Geoffrey's truck, wings as wide as the cab and in that same instant it was silently gone. In the woods at the edge of the clearing I can hear birds among the trees, and wish I knew their calls.

Once, when I summered in Chapel Hill, a mockingbird near my room spent part of the afternoons calling out the sounds of an ice cream truck, police sirens and occasionally shouts of boys playing baseball in the street. At Sagehen Creek Mark and his assistant tied fine-meshed nets between the trees to capture tiny songbirds. They needed a magnifying glass to fix the tiny bands to their legs. The birds remained still, Mark's hand closed around the body while an assistant clipped the band around the toothpick of a leg. In flight they were indistinguishable from each other, but when captured, there appeared yellow wings and throats, black caps, and rich brown backs.

Six years ago, Garry Sayer wrote to me: *Purple bruised sky, leafless trees bent in the strong wind, pheasants and rooks about their earth-picking business and the odd buzzard and hawk riding the air.* Everything about Dorset is captured in his words.

Egrets stalk the marsh, white question marks among the reeds. They lift their legs a millimeter at a time, their heads motionless, waiting for some movement in the water. In the brilliant green rice fields they are single brush strokes.

The sedge wren weighs only nine grams, about the weight of six paper clips. A mottled brown, its heart beats seven times faster than a human heart. There are other wrens: the rock wren, the canyon wren, the Pacific wren, the marsh wren, and the house wren, a miniature bird with a white throat.

Its heart is no bigger than the tip of my little finger, yet it throbs insistently, propelling the tiny bird in flight into hedges, through the branches of trees, its miniscule claws suddenly grasping an oak twig. It would take three hundred such hearts to make up the mass of mine.

My younger brother's heart has struggled once, and now struggles again, a valve opening and closing erratically. I think of the wren's heart, the heart of the merganser, the heart of the egret that beats in a stillness that is complete and I think of my brother's heart, surrounded by muscle and flesh, struggling to maintain a rhythm that will enable him to, once again, snowshoe into the mountains in the dead of winter.

There was a bird researcher at Sagehen Creek who shot sparrows with a .22, keeping the tiny carcasses for study. I thought of bird hearts that had been stilled and wondered if, somehow, those hearts could have been installed in my brother's heart, transplanted into the valve that was erratic, filling the void that would not work correctly. But, of course, those hearts beat seven times faster than his heart. No chance that there would be a match.

It was strange, she said, that she had to kill the birds to study their lives. There were, she said, thousands of study skins in museums. By examining the skins of the birds she had shot, she had been able to determine that a sparrow on the coast was different from the sparrows in the inland valleys and mountains.

Audubon shot some of the birds that he painted so that he could examine them at close hand. Audubon hired a teenage boy to paint the riverbanks for him. I imagine that boy, drifting down the river, into a wilderness that had barely been touched by white men. Audubon told of seeing a flock of passenger pigeons that passed overhead. "The air was literally filled with pigeons; the light of noon-day sun was obscured as by an eclipse."

They continued to blot out the sky for the fifty-five miles it took to reach St. Louis. He reported that they blotted out the sun for the next three days. Millions of birds. None of them are left.

There are no more Bickfords. The only Hills left are my brother and I, and, of course, our children. In the back yard at Grandpa Bickford's house in Wyanet, there was a Martin house. A miniature mansion, it was several stories high, on a raised post with multiple entry holes to the nesting rooms, an apartment house for birds. The martins darted toward it, coming to a sudden stop on the peg outside a hole and then disappeared inside.

Grandpa Bickford told me that the birds wintered in Brazil, and I got out my Goode's School Atlas and traced a line south from Illinois, to the Gulf of Mexico and beyond, down to the South American continent until it reached Brazil. The legend in the corner of the map told me that they had flown five thousand miles.

They come every summer, he said. Same birds come back, and the mother and father bird are the same, stuck with each other. I wondered at his verb.

The martins were swallows, feeding in the air, taking beetles, flies, damsel flies, midges, bees, cicadas, flying ants, butterflies and moths, grasshoppers and wasps. They drank from ponds, skimming along the surface to take a beak of water in full flight. Their weight, I found out, was a mere 1.9 ounces. Less than two first class letters. How small was this brain that remembered a martin house in my grandfather's back yard, five thousand miles from where they had started? What kind of a heart kept beating five hundred times a minute as they flew six hundred miles across the open water of the Gulf of Mexico?

I sat on the grass between the house and the barn and watched them darting and swooping in the evening air. What kind of eyesight and physical prowess did it take to snatch a flying wasp or a cicada moving from one tree to another?

A half century later I stood in a riffle on the Feather River, casting for a steelhead. The water pulled at my legs and I was suddenly conscious of swallows skimming the surface, taking insects There were dozens of them, an intricate dance in the air and I stopped casting, watching, wondering how many insects they needed to fuel the metabolism of their tiny bodies.

This morning's crow waited at the top of the driveway. He

rose, lifting himself into the oak tree and he yelled at me, insistent, over and over. Another crow called from across the canyon. I have seen them descend in a circular cloud, falling into the trees like a black breath, dark shapes filling the branches, moving against the dusk. There seem to be more crows than there used to be, picking at things in the road, rowing silently overhead, distinct against the pale summer blue, hopping across the street, lifting suddenly when the car is almost upon them, dive-bombing a hawk that hovers over the ridge, harrowing it off.

Crows learn to recognize people. Did this morning's crow know me, know I was getting into my truck? Was it shouting at me to leave something behind? Accusing me of disrupting some morning crow ritual?

There are stellar jays in the Nelson Creek canyon, hawks and kestrels hover over the sagebrush flats, seagulls circle the school at lunch and swoop inside the rim of the stadium.

But crows stay close to my house, call out in the evening when I sit on the patio with a drink, rise into the oaks at dawn, and they are not silent. They make themselves known.

"Here I am!" they shout. Over and over.

I met a priest at Eleanor Hopewell's shop in Berkeley. He was from Brazil, and I told him about the purple martins that flew from Brazil to my grandfather's house in Illinois.

"Do you know where in Brazil?" he asked.

"No, I do not."

"No immigration, no passports, no customs, no borders," he said.

"But it's amazing that they could go all that distance to find the same back garden each year," I said.

Perhaps not, he replied.

I go to the gym in the early morning, and walk aimlessly on the treadmill, setting it at an incline that will exercise my heart, increasing the speed as I walk. The machine monitors my heart rate, tells me when I am reaching too far. But it is nothing compared to the heart rate of birds. I am a sloth compared to them. My older brother died of a heart attack, a massive jolt that stopped him at his desk one morning, and then I discovered that the Hill men had a history of exploding hearts. Only my father, Ėho succumbed to tuberculosis, escaped. So, I hike along the North Fork of the Yuba, climbing over rocks, careful not to slip, feeling my heart race faster when I cast toward a long race, and later, in a cabin on the edge of the river, I drink a scotch and the sound of the river fills the air. Paul and I are a long way from our grandfather's back yard. Below me, swifts skim the surface of the stream, picking insects out of the air. Perhaps birds live a life as long as mine, only at a faster pace.

IV
Dogs

IN THE LOBBY of the post office was an old black dog. It lay next to the door, waiting. At the counter was an old man, belly sagging over his belt, wearing an orange tee shirt, and when he opened the door the dog got up, and he said, "hey, buddy," and the dog went before him and I watched them cross the parking lot, the dog leading the way to the truck. An old man and his old dog.

Jim Harrison wrote in a poem, "How can this dog on the cushion at my feet have passed me in the continuum of age," and I guess that the man in the orange tee shirt is in his seventies and perhaps the dog is in its eighties. But it looks back at him to make sure he is following.

In the early morning darkness there is no birdsong, no sound, only the whirring of the pump and the memory of another morning. And another black dog on a beach in the blackness of morning, disappearing when the ball was thrown, the sound of the sea to the left, and the dog came out of the darkness to drop the ball at my feet and waited, vibrating, until I threw it again. And for those moments, she was my dog, came to me, wet and eager, and when we went back to the cabin where others were waking, Bella's owner waited for us on the deck, hair drawn back, wrapped in a blanket.

The dog rubbed against her legs. She was not my dog again.

Once I took her out to a beach in West Marin. This time it was an afternoon gathering of women and the dog would be a nuisance, so I took her. She rode in my truck, sitting in the passenger seat as if she were my companion, watching out the window for other trucks or cars, and when we got to the beach she ran into the water, ran again and again for the tennis ball and then came to me, shook herself and we rode back together. I stopped at a bar in Forest Knolls and said to her, "Stay here. Watch the truck. Don't let anybody in the cab. Drive off if they threaten you," and she moved over into the driver's seat.

When we got back to the house I said to her, "You don't need to tell anybody I stopped for a scotch. Remember. You're my dog. I'm loaning you to these people. Be nice to them. I won't be far away."

She didn't say anything. That's the way with dogs. They keep their thoughts to themselves. I imagine the first time the greyhounds ran with the Sheik's horses on the sands of Arabia. They ran flat out, pacing the horses, and they were lean and graceful and at night a pile of them surrounded the queen, were her blanket when the desert temperature dropped precipitously. Perhaps they talked among themselves about the vastness of the desert, or the fruitlessness of racing horses toward some unseen goal.

When our dog, Quincy, began to lose his senses, his sight became vague and his hearing was such that he heard only the slamming of doors or the shouting of children, and he began to lash out at unseen dangers. Someone approached him from behind and tried to scratch his ears and he was surprised, had not heard them or seen them, lashed out at what he didn't know was there. I sympathized with him No one else did. But I knew that feeling of someone catching you by surprise, sneaking up on you with good intentions, but there was no way to know that the intentions were good. Beware! I did not lash out, but he did. And he was banished during parties, sent to a locked room. Not your fault, I told him. He kept his thoughts to himself.

And the time came when I took him to the vet. His hips had displaced, he was in obvious pain and the vet said, "He's unraveling. I can stitch him up again with drugs but it's no hope for him. Would you like me to put him down?"

"No," I said. "He's my responsibility." And I took him to the humane society, and we sat in the little reception room. He sat at my feet, looking quite fit, and I stroked him and then they came for him and I went out to the truck and sat in the seat and cried. I did not cry for my father. I did not cry for my older brother. Why did I cry for a dog that bit children, had scabrous lesions on his back, was no longer nice to anyone who bent to stroke his neck?

When he was younger and good with children we took him to the groomer where he was bathed and clipped so that his little schnauzer face had tufted eyebrows and a bearded look, but his coat was short. He was quite stylish. We went to the groomer to bring him home and Quincy was nervous, resisted the leash, growled at me. The groomer said nothing, but when we got home we found a red mark where the groomer's clippers had made a cut in his skin. The next time we left him, when we came back we were met by the woman with a bandage on her hand and Quincy was only half clipped. "I don't ever want to see that dog again," she said. But it was hardly the dog's fault. The sound of the clippers had brought back the memory of being injured and he lashed out at the offending noise. From then on, I had to groom him. I cinched a canvas belt around his muzzle so he couldn't bite me, held him with his neck in my armpit while I clipped him. He struggled, growled, frothed at the mouth, and when we were done he ran to the far side of the patio, turned and looked at me with distrust. Eventually he learned to tolerate the act of grooming, but there was, imprinted in his memory, the pain associated with the buzz of the clippers.

A long time ago, when I was a teenager, I went up to Oakland Camp in the Sierras in the winter. I took the Budd Car, a single unit Western Pacific diesel that went up the Feather River Canyon, and I stayed with Charlie Way and his wife. Charlie was the caretaker of Oakland camp, and I had worked for Charlie for three summers. That fall two dogs had come into camp, ragged, half-starved, and Charlie had managed to collect them, made them a kennel in his workshop, and put an ad in the Feather River Bulletin, the weekly newspaper in Quincy. The call came from a bear hunter. He was beside himself with joy. Charlie had found his two bear dogs, and he came for them, presented Charlie with a package of bear meat, roasts and chops and sausage. He offered money, but Charlie said no, it wasn't necessary. He would not take money for finding another man's dogs.

I was there when the man came. The dogs were, by then, sleek. Charlie had fed them and groomed them. Charlie was from Alabama, where hunting dogs were cherished. When the owner came, the dogs did not show any excitement. They followed him to his truck obediently. They were dogs that did not shy at the blast of a gun; those dogs went quietly into the back of the hunter's truck.

That afternoon Charlie's wife marinated the bear roast and that night the gamey meat fell off the bone onto our plates.

WHEN MY BROTHER Paul was the forest service ranger at a guard station on the Carissa plains east of San Luis Obispo, he took his dog with him, hunting bobcats. He asked me if I wanted to go with him. When I asked him how long it would take, he said, "As long as it takes. If he gets on the scent we follow him, and maybe it's an hour and maybe it's four hours, and maybe it's all night." I decided against it. Paul and his dog left in the afternoon and we didn't see them until the next morning. Paul posed for a photo against the fence of the guard station holding the bobcat. Mike sat at his leg, looking unconcerned.

He came across the ford, his horse stepping carefully through the water, and stopped in front of the house. Heat radiated from the bare earth and insects crackled in the single live oak that shaded the corner of the house. Mike dropped off the porch and went out to meet him. What struck me was that when Mike got to the horse and rider, he turned and sat next to the horse, as if he belonged there.

It was Jack Callahan, the foreman for the Avenales Land and Cattle Company. Paul was the ranger at the Avenales Guard Station for the forest service, a tiny house eleven miles inside the locked ranch gate, across a shallow ford on the headwaters of the Salinas river. It was the house where his oldest son would be born. Callahan sat there, his lined face dark under his beat-up Stetson. The horse shifted easily.

"Hot."

Callahan wasn't given to a lot of talk.

"Sure is."

Callahan looked down at Mike, studied him carefully.

"That's a good dog," he said.

"We think so," Paul said. "He's good with children. He'll make a good family dog."

Callahan looked at Paul, then at the dog.

"You mind if I borrow him for a few hours?"

"What for?"

"I got some cattle up the arroyo and I thought maybe I could use some help."

"He's not trained. Never herded sheep or cattle."

Callahan studied the dog. It sat next to the horse, just off from the front legs, and it was studying Callahan, head canted upwards.

"He's a likely looking dog. I believe he would be a help. That is," he added, "if you'd be willing to loan him out."

"Be my guest."

Callahan nodded, touched the brim of his hat and turned the horse. He whistled and Mike trotted after him, as if Callahan had owned him all of his life. I watched the horse go through the water, Mike splashing after him, and then, as they went up the far bank, Mike stopped to shake himself, looked back at Paul as if to say, I won't be long, and trotted off after the horse and rider.

We didn't think much more about it that afternoon. Callahan would take care of Mike, that much we knew.

The sun was slanting across the Sierra Madres, the air cooling when we heard the horse and when we stepped out onto the porch Callahan was coming across the ford, Mike trailing just behind. Callahan reined in a few yards off and the horse stood there, snorting. Mike sat next to the horse in the same spot he had taken nearly four hours before.

"He's a good cow dog," Callahan said.

"He's never worked cattle," Paul said.

"Don't matter. It's in their blood. He did OK for a first time out." He touched the brim of his hat again.

"I'm much obliged," he said. He started to turn the horse and then paused, turning back in the saddle to face us. "You ever decide to go someplace, I'd be happy to take that dog," he said.

"Not much chance of that," Paul said. "We like him too much."

"Be that as it may," Callahan said, "whatever you do, don't ever take that dog to the city." He kicked the horse and it went down the shallow incline into the water, hooves clattering against the rocks. Mike looked at the departing horse, looked at Paul, and then came up onto the porch.

Callahan never mentioned the dog again, nor asked to borrow him. A year later Paul took another post at a Job Corps camp in the Mendocino Forest and they lived in a compound of ten-wides at Alder Springs and several years later Lyndon Johnson's Great Society began to unravel and Paul ended up at the Regional office in San Francisco. He bought a house in a tract in a Petaluma suburb and he rode the Greyhound to work every morning. Mike stayed in the fenced yard all day.

Paul came home one evening from a family outing and spotted Mike's body next to highway 101, the two-lane highway that bisected Petaluma. Somehow Mike had found his way there and perhaps he'd spotted some cows across the road or maybe he decided to try to head one of those cars, but all Paul could think of was Callahan telling him, "don't ever take that dog to the city."

But they had taken Mike to the city and Paul thought, why didn't I give him to Callahan but of course they weren't going to the city when they left Avenales. They were going to the Mendocino where Mike could roam among the pines and the yard wasn't fenced, and traffic was the occasional forest service truck laboring up the grade toward the Hoopa reservation.

Still, Callahan's words haunted Paul. He got another dog, and he told me, "This one is an idiot." He was a leaper. You could see his head pop up over the six-foot fence when you walked past, like some sort of Jack-in-the-box toy, bouncing up along the fence as you moved forward, but he wasn't the kind of dog that Callahan would have looked at and said, "That's a likely looking dog."

WHEN I WAS NINE we had a dog. In the Illinois winter Pam, a black cocker spaniel, would play with my brother Paul and me in the snow-covered vacant lot next door. And when my mother called us to supper we came in the kitchen door where we shed our snowsuits and galoshes and mittens and caps. I can still remember the smell of wet wool, a smell that hung in the cloakroom at school, and in the service porches of houses. And then we put Pam on her back, pulled the pieces of ice that were imbedded between her toes while she whimpered. Pam smelled of wet fur and the musk of winter. The kitchen was warm from the coal stove where my mother was making dinner and we rubbed Pam with old towels. That spring my father, who was a teacher at the local high school, was diagnosed with tuberculosis and he went off to a magic mountain in New Mexico. My two brothers and my mother and I went off to California to live with her aunt and uncle. But Pam couldn't go with us. We took her to the house of my grandfather's brother, Uncle Sam, a tiny man with a tiny fireplug wife. He worked at the high school in Sycamore and I remember going with him one morning and being allowed to raise the American flag in front of the high school.

I took a last photograph of Paul with Pam, using my Brownie box camera. He stands in the driveway holding up some sort of a treat and Pam holds her head toward it. All I remember of Pam were those moments in the kitchen when I picked ice from between her toes. I have no memory of her being a family dog, lying on our bed at night, or playing with us in the summer heat. Only her whimpering protests as we pried the ice from between her toes.

SHORTY WAS A FIREPLUG of a man who lived in a house with dogs. I could never figure out how many dogs there were. They were rangy dogs that climbed onto the ratty furniture, pissed on the cracked and torn linoleum and barked incessantly at strangers. His dogs had the look of coyotes, lean, crawling over each other, high-pitched yips punctuating the air. Empty dog food cans lay scattered on the floor and the house smelled like a kennel.

Shorty worked as a handy-man, carpenter, jack-of-all-trades at Oakland Camp, lived in his ramshackle, uncompleted house on the road to camp and was an ex-con. Except for the occasional stay in the Plumas County jail. What his crimes were I never knew. He had been a boxer and had a checkerboard past that he only hinted at.

He set out fishing lines on Spanish Creek, tying lengths of monofilament to branches overhanging the stream, hooks baited with bunches of worms drifting in the current He came back the next day, harvested the trout that drifted at the ends of the taut lines and took them into Quincy, trading them to the cooks at Moon's Bar and Grill, a trout for each bottle of beer.

Shorty had a Hudson Hornet, a powerful bulbous sedan and he sat on a pillow, barely peering over the top of the steering wheel. Once, on a trip to Reno, he pulled out to pass a speeding Cadillac. Out of a dip in the highway ahead of us rose the snout of a logging truck and I thought he would hit the brakes, but he stomped on the accelerator and at the same time pulled on a wire that stuck out from the dashboard. The car jerked, slammed forward and we roared past the startled Caddy driver, dodging back into the lane just in time to miss the oncoming logger.

Fuck 'em all! Shorty shouted. He had wired an old hair dryer to the open carburetor of the Hudson and it shot a blast of hot air into the gasoline mixture, a crude supercharger. Fuck 'em all, he shouted, bouncing on the cushion beneath him. I was paralyzed by the near miss.

His dogs had the look of feral animals. Shorty had some of that look, too. It was the summer of 1953. The next summer when I came back to work at Oakland Camp, Shorty was not there. His house was empty, the tarpaper still peeling off the sides. There were no dogs.

OUR CHILDREN have had dogs. Graham, the youngest has had more than the others. Yukon, a rangy half malamute, half wolf that stood on top of his dog house when it began to snow. "He can run thirty miles an hour," Graham told me.

"How do you know that?"

"I took my Bronco down onto the beach and he kept up with me until I reached thirty." Yukon was a dog that needed to run full out, and Graham realized that keeping him in a Victorian house with a limited yard was no longer an option. He found Yukon a home on a ranch near Blue Lake.

Snuffy was a dog that had no visible redeeming qualities. He was an old dog and the old man who owned him died. The son took him to the police, and Graham, who was a policeman at the time, couldn't stomach seeing the old dog put down. He brought him home to the house he shared with Bob. But Snuffy tried to chew his way out of the house, destroying the door jamb. He shook, much like one of those motel beds where you put a quarter in and the bed vibrates, but you didn't have to put a quarter into Snuffy. One tooth stuck out of the side of his mouth, giving him a permanently nasty grin. He fixated on cats, tried repeatedly to run away. "He's looking for the old man," Graham said. "You can't blame him." When it became apparent that the dog could not be left alone when Graham pulled a midnight to six shift, Graham put him in the back seat of the police cruiser. He pinned a "junior policeman" badge onto Snuffy's collar. "He's an undercover dog," Graham said.

Snuffy replaced a dog named Boozer, part Doberman, part Rotweiler, that Graham found as a teenager. He knew that he couldn't bring the dog to our house where my wife harbored a deep fear of large dogs. So he had girls at his high school take the dog home each night, but when he ran out of girls, the dog appeared in our house. Banished, it went off to live with his brother at college, but there it menaced diners at sidewalk tables in Berkeley and eventually it was adopted by a beer truck driver who wanted a dog that looked fierce to guard his truck while he made deliveries in the worst parts of Oakland. It was a gentle dog that meant no one harm.

And there was Maya.

Crossing the Van Duzen at first light. There is a thin skin of ice on the bridge and the river looks like irregular lead sheets, winding between gravel bars. Fields are white with thick frost, black cattle huddled next to the fence along the highway. In the headlights a yellow cat darts from under Graham's parked truck. The Eel is wide and flat and shivers in the morning wind. It took a long time this morning for the windshield to thaw, the wipers stripping a sheet of wet ice off to one side. Smoke from a chimney bellies, a long tongue of gray held to the ground by the cold air, filtering through the trees. Fishermen report that sea lions have come up the mouth of the Eel all the way to Scotia to feast on steelhead and salmon. Kill the fuckers said Tim, Just bring along a high-powered pistol and shoot the fuckers when they come up. But it's the logging that did in the great runs, silting the spawning beds, closing off creeks, and now there is little water, so few storms this year that you could easily wade the Van Duzen above the 101 bridge. It should be shoulder deep, surging with winter rain.

This morning I am going to Fortuna to buy breakfast: eggs and sausage and bread and juice. My son's Rio Dell house will not come alive for another hour. Only the dog, Maya, and I are awake. Maya rides with me to the store and when we get back, I read a book at the kitchen table, pausing now and then to read a paragraph to the dog. When I do, she raises her head, brown eyes liquid and alert. She does not blink. It occurs to me that perhaps dogs do not blink. Maya is part heeler and her head is flat and she raises it so I can rub behind her ears. I would steal you, Maya, I say to her, but you belong to my son and his family.

Graham and I have made plans to go fishing this summer. Later in the morning he will talk with one of his officers. A pit bull has killed an alpaca and a goat and two cats and he is telling Josh that he will have to shoot it.

"If you're uncomfortable with that, let me know and I'll come down," he says. He is matter-of-fact about it. I have a photograph of Graham making a roll cast on a beaver pond on Graeagle Creek. He must have been about ten years old when I took that photo. The man who stands in his kitchen, talking to one of his police officers bears no resemblance to that kid. Like insects that come to the surface of the river and shed their cases, whirling up into the air, we change. We become something else. There is a photograph of my brother and me on a horse at Uncle Earl's farm. I must have been about thirteen. This year I will turn seventy-two. I, too, have become someone else.

I read a poem from Robert Penn Warren's *Selected Poems* to Maya. The lines are, "Long ago, in Kentucky, I, a boy, stood/ by a dirt road, in first dark, and heard/the great geese hoot northward."

Maya seems to listen. But Maya doesn't know anything about being ten years old, or at least I don't think she does. One of my grandsons, Nathaniel, is ten years old. One afternoon in his back yard he pointed to the sky and said, "Look, Poppa!" and I looked up and a vee of snow geese was heading north. I had not recognized their cries, but Nathaniel had, like Warren, heard them. "They're back," Nathaniel had said.

When I look back at what I have written, I realize that there is something here that Maya cannot know. Each of these things, the first light on the Van Duzen, the Safeway store in Fortuna, the smoke sliding down a roof, Graham as a boy and Graham as a man, the dog next to the breakfast table in a house where the only sound is the hum of the refrigerator—all of these are parts of my memory. And when I read something, those things will be part of what I read. Warren writes of a log cabin in the Kentucky wilderness; the smoke slides down the roof of that cabin where a young Audubon will spend the night and it is the smoke that I saw on my way to the store that morning, the ice melting on the windshield. When Nathaniel is my age and he reads that poem, the smoke that he will see will be a different smoke. Neither of them will be the smoke in Warren's poem.

Nathaniel will, if he reads Warren's lines about the geese, recall the snow geese in the empty rice fields south of Chico, the clouds of geese lifting from the stubble, and the afternoon when he pointed out the faintly honking vee far above our heads. Although he will be separated from Warren's experience by several thousand miles and nearly a century, he will be closer to Warren's image than most who read the poem. He will bring to those words the geese that are in his memory.

THIS MORNING I was awakened by the coyotes. There was a chorus of trilling and sharp barks tumbling into each other and then silence. Shorty and Charlie Way and Snuffy and Yukon and Quincy and Bella are gone. Paul's dog was run over by a car on highway 101. Pam and the Illinois winters with snow and ice and a long trudge to the brick faced elementary school have faded. Gary and his coyote have slipped off the raft. The heron that came down out of the tangle of trees to stab at the fish in his tiny ponds no longer comes. Maya remains, patient, but is now older than I am. Geoff's family dog has gone from a frantic thing that barked at airplanes and chased squirrels that were seventy feet above her into a quiet dog that ignores the chickens feeding on the lawn.

When we came to California Aunt Edna and Uncle Howard had a dog. Watch was a wire-haired terrier, an alert dog whose name suited him. Jack Winslett was a friend of theirs. He was in the army. Major Winslett. We were told to address him as Major. He had a wife and two girls, both of whom were spoiled. They were fawned over by the major and his wife and Georgine was rough with Watch and he bit her. Not seriously, but he drew blood and Major Winslett insisted that Watch be taken away for observation. Watch was taken to a place where there were other dogs and he caught distemper and died. Uncle Howard was angry, but he controlled his temper. Barely. After all, it was war time and Winslett was a major in the army. But Major Winslett was an arrogant bastard. If you believed him, he was General MacArthur's personal assistant in Tokyo. Paul and I didn't believe him. And one night at the dinner table, he waxed eloquent about how ships that sank in the Pacific sank only to the depth where their displacement equaled the pressure of the ocean. My older brother suddenly spoke up.

"That's nonsense," he said, and a silence settled over the table. There were eleven of us at that table: Aunt Edna and Uncle Howard, my mother, her sister Laura, us three boys, Eva Baer who worked with Aunt Laura and Mr. Brown who worked in Breuner's department store too, Winslett and a sailor that Uncle Howard had picked up on the ferry on the way home from work. Ollie Melvin, the sailor who had been invited to dinner by Uncle Howard asked for the potatoes. They came to him as if they were precious glass.

"You don't know what you're talking about," my brother said. Ronald was seventeen, but he was a whiz at science and mathematics and he had had enough of Jack Winslett's bullshit. Paul and I sat, transfixed. I thought that lightning would strike Ronald. I do not remember how that evening ended, but the man who had caused the death of Watch had been put in his place. From that point on, Paul and I relegated Ronald to the world of adults. He was no longer our older brother, sleeping in the windowless room with us in the basement. He had put a stake through the heart of an adult who deserved it.

Dogs. They are tied outside the coffee shop in Fairfax, and I cannot pass one without stopping to touch its head. If there is an owner I ask if I can give the dog a treat, and if the answer is yes, I reach into my pocket for a beef pupper-oni. I carried them for Bella, the black lab that I sometimes was allowed to walk in the park in the early morning. Half a pupperoni in one hand, half in the other, and she knew that there were two treats. She lay outside the window of the coffee shop, raising her head to those who paused to stroke her. When I have coffee in the cafe in the morning, there is an emptiness where she lay next to the window.

Moon's had a bar dog. She was fat from treats dropped by regulars, bits of beef jerky, French fries. She moved slowly. Bar dogs were dogs that spent a lot of time dozing. Dogs that were not about to bite anyone, even the careless drinker who accidentally stepped on them. Dogs with the unlikely name of Speedy or Elmer. Dogs that had no bark, or had decided not to bark again, not even when bar stools crashed around them and beer steins bounced off the walls. Never small dogs that might get squashed by a staggering drunk. Dogs big enough to shed the wandering foot of a man three sheets to the wind. Dogs that got scratched behind the ears by men who were by themselves at the bar and had no chance of finding anyone who would scratch them behind the ears. I do not remember the name of Moon's bar dog. She was simply a part of the furniture. She was there, beneath the bar stools and there at the end of the evening. She did not drink beer. She did not try to curry favor from anyone. She was herself. Nobody in particular.

WAITING. An old dog is tied to the lamp post. An old dog face, resigned, patient, not much movement. I know what's that like. Save your energy, old dog. It turns its head, looks at me and I go outside to my bike, get a doggie treat for the old dog, bring it to him, hold it in my open palm beneath his muzzle and he noses it, reluctantly takes it; perhaps he's been told not to take treats from strangers. Ordinarily I would ask the owner if I could give the dog something, but there is no one near, and no one in the coffee shop that resembles a dog owner. Whatever that looks like. You're a good old dog, I say, and the dog doesn't reply. He doesn't move his head, just waits.

I go back in, take my place at the counter next to the window where I can watch him. He waits. He has waited a great deal in his life. I have waited, too.

Waited in the car for the shopping trip to be over, waited in an Adirondack chair in the back patio for the sun to go off the mountain. Waited while the clock in the classroom ticked the last minutes before dismissal, waited while the surgeon took off his gloves and came to tell me that the blockage in my heart was still there. Waited while the Chancellor read through the names in the hot sun in Memorial Stadium until he came to my name. Waited for the wind to die on the North Fork so that I could cast again. Waited while the captain shuffled my papers and then said that I was not qualified to be a soldier. I waited in Bushrod Center for ten o'clock so I could close the gym, shoo out the last of the basketball players and lock the doors. I waited at the path below the girls' tents at Oakland camp for Carolyn. I am waiting for October to come again.

I would steal that old dog. If I were a dog stealer. He and I would wait together. For whatever it is that waits for us.

V
What Is True

DANCING THE AVENUE. It is 1960 and I am once again walking up MacArthur Boulevard with a young woman, one that I have fallen in love with, and we stop in a bar. It is a cement block bar, like all of the others in this working class neighborhood. Behind us is the Chevrolet truck plant and there are men working the night shift, the long lines carrying truck chassis and engines and fenders and the workers live in small houses that rise on the slope east of the boulevard. We enter the bar. It is the kind of place where men drink shots and beer and we order two beers and put a quarter in the juke box and punch several numbers and then we dance and one of the men says, "Way to go!" and we dance slowly, pressing against each other, until the song is finished.

When the beer and the songs are finished we go out into the night and go to the bar in the next block. We call it "dancing the avenue." It is sixty years ago. The Chevrolet truck plant is no longer there. The bars have grids of steel on the windows. Young men lounge on the corners, calling out to passing cars, and it feels dangerous. But I can feel the music, dancing close to her, and the years melt away.

Dancing the avenue.

A HUNDRED CREEKS. At dusk, I stand on the road looking down into the canyon and the light has gone and it is only an inky black below me with the sound of the creek somewhere below, so deep I do not know where it is, running over stones and beneath the stones and deeper even than that, so deep I cannot measure.

An egret stands at the edge of the river at dark. Water swirls around its legs. It seems oblivious to the water, waiting for something, perhaps nothing. The water that touches the yellow legs eddies, joins the current where it will go for a hundred miles to the sea and it will mix with the water that has come from a hundred creeks and it will flow into the sea and it will become part of the vastness and some of it will rise and become grey rain squalls that approach a ship or beat across a beach, perhaps in some far-off land where the word for egret is *aigrette* or *tsiknias*. And some of it will rise and come across the land again and will fall as rain on the tin roof of a cabin or pool on the highway or fall as snow, drifting in great soft flakes to join the river and it will be impossible to measure which snowflake touched the leg of the egret or which water that drums on the roof went to the sea that night.

The long tongues of Tomales Bay are like strips of steel in the morning light. The hills to the west are blots of grey and above them is a halo of pastel: peach and lemon. The earth turns slowly and the sun suddenly breaks on the bay and the grasses are alight, as if on fire for an instant. I wait for birds. I have coffee in Pt. Reyes Station and at the bakery buy a pastry made with soft croissant dough, filled with almond that tastes like chocolate. I pass White House pool where, a century ago, children played at the edge of the water and men in suits and straw hats fished for salmon and women in long dresses with parasols talked. A hundred years ago is not a long time.

OCTOBER SILENCE. It is a low-slung cabin with a rusted tin roof, a weathered screen door and a sloping wooden floor. There is a heater in the wall, and a gas flame bubbles from a propane tank outside and the shower and toilet are in a lean-to scabbed onto the north wall. Rain drums on the roof. It began to rain after midnight and now at four o'clock it has slowed to a soft beat. In the afternoon the river was dark green, half of the water in shadow, the other half still lit by the sun.

Once again I am writing about the sun going off the mountain. It's evening and the shadows deepen and the folds of the mountain grow dark, and I think of other folds that darkened: Nelson Creek where the shadows closed over the water and trout rose in the half-dark and Art Morris and I climbed out, scrabbling up the steep canyon wall, and sat in the dusk on the edge of the graveled road to smoke a cigarette. I remember the Zippo lighter that was burnished silver and flared in the dark, and the cigarettes glowed and we smoked in silence while we caught our breath. We looked down where it was now black and the creek bubbled over stones somewhere below us.

We climbed out of English Bar at dark. We fished until we could not see the fly, struck at the sound of rising trout, and then crawled up the trail on hands and knees. The trail was in an old creek bed, filled with rocks and roots and at some point Art made a sound like a rattlesnake and we froze. Steve Walker was between me and Art and he waited and then said, "Fuck you, Morris!" and Art laughed. But we knew the snakes would come to the open warm earth for the night and when we got to the top of the ridge it was pitch black. There was my '39 Ford with a windshield that cranked out so we could put our rods through it into the car. We were relieved. But we never said that we were relieved. We were in our twenties and that wasn't something that twenty-five-year-old men admitted to in those days.

I remember stumbling down out of Tollgate Creek in the dark, seeing the lights of Oakland Camp below me and using those lights as a guide. I can no longer do that. I can no longer fish until it is black.

Once, not long ago on Nelson Creek, I waited at the base of the trail that rises up to where the truck was parked, and Geoffrey was somewhere upstream, still fishing. The light failed, the stream grew indistinct and I was pissed off. "Come on," I said out loud, and I called out to him but there was no answer. We had no flashlight and I waited, counting the minutes and then he materialized, not ten yards from me, wading across the stream; we climbed up wordlessly and I remembered fishing on Spanish Creek thirty years before until it was too dark to see, coming back through the railroad tunnel, so black I could not see my hand in front of my face. There were small islands of elephant ears that hung over the water and big browns waited under them, but we knew they were nocturnal feeders so we fished until we couldn't see the fly; then we came up to the railroad tracks and walked in the blackness through the two tunnels back to camp.

The harvest moon is rising in the east this evening. The mountain is a black outline and I think of other evenings: the roadhouse at Mt. Tomba and a scotch at the bar. Outside the temperature would be dropping. October light is not far off. The autumnal equinox arrives in a week. It will be exactly half way between the longest day of the year and the shortest day. The light goes off the mountain earlier now and it is dark when I rise in the morning. The temperature in the creeks will drop and the trout will have one last feeding frenzy before they slip into their winter slowness.

You ask what is true. I think of my father, who laid a spirit level on the board and asked, "Is it true?" That was the carpenter's word. He was a meticulous man, with drafts-man's hands and no detail was missed. There was no room for carelessness in his world. I cannot lay the spirit level on those rivers and creeks. Unlike the wood my father fastened together, they are fluid, change with the seasons, and are made of things that are hard to measure: the sound of water over stones, the flash of something white beneath the green surface. Those streams are a constant in my life, but I cannot hold them. I feel them pulling at my thighs, plunge my hands into them, hear them at night from beyond the cabin walls. I have listened to rain drum on the surface and watched ice craze the edges. One midnight I watched black women in flowing white dresses and turbans bending in prayer at the edge of the Mississippi, its wide flat blackness rolling silently before them. Once the sun set on the Sacramento and for an instant the river was on fire. I have plunged into icy creeks on a hot July day and emerged, gasping. I have asked my sons to drop my ashes off the Nelson Point Bridge. I can see the ashes floating down toward the dark green water. I had lunch on that bridge once. I danced on the warped wooden boards to music from my truck radio. The creek danced below me. True story.

TOLLGATE CREEK, so tiny I can step over it. It pools below rocks under the willows and there are small bright trout in it. Dennis Curran and I came all the way down Tollgate in 1954, starting high on Mt Hough, sliding down wet rocks, drop-ping into pools, looking for the source of the grubs that had shown up in the strainer in the Oakland Camp water system. We found the carcass of the deer a hundred yards above the water tank, a few hundred yards from camp. But we had experienced every foot of that tiny stream. Art took the tip section of his fly rod, tied a short piece of leader to it and dangled a fly under the willows. The water suddenly exploded as a trout rose to take it.

Bucks Creek spills out into the North Fork of the Feather just above Bucks powerhouse. It rises steeply, rocks the size of Volkswagens, white water tumbling into green pools. Stand in one pool and fish the one above, the water at eye level. Once I dislocated my shoulder on Bucks Creek and Art and his dad drove me into Oroville to have it re-set. In the emergency room was a young man, still hammered, with criss-cross marks on his face where he had run his motorcycle into the backstop of the Little League baseball park. He waited, comatose, while I had my shoulder reset.

Once I surprised a rattlesnake in the shadow of one of those huge rocks.

Soldier Creek is tiny, north of Yellow Creek, and Sheepheaven Creek is only three-quarters of a mile long before it disappears in the lava on the eastern slope of Mt. Shasta.

Sagehen Creek wanders through a small valley that is home to the University of California's field research station where the first photographs were made of trout spawning. Geoffrey spent several summers there. Beavers have worked that stream, and slow pools interrupt the creek periodically. Geoffrey lived in Starker Leopold's summer cabin, a pot bellied wood stove in the center of the single room.

Sayles Canyon Creek empties into the Yuba and there are rainbow, brown and brook trout in the miniature pools. At night from the Newby's cabin you can hear the creek tumbling below.

Gance Creek, in the high desert of Nevada is host to the Humboldt cutthroat trout, a unique fish that survives extremely high temperatures and freezing winters in a creek that dribbles between thorny bushes and buck brush, the banks trampled by cattle that have created an acidity that would kill any other fish. The Humboldt trout survive.

Graham and I fished a miniscule Maine creek with Eleanor's great uncle, who filled his pockets with tiny brook trout and they were fried whole, head and all, eaten like French fries.

Ranchers carried milk cans with fingerling trout to remote streams, planting them so that outriders could have fresh trout for supper. At the battle of Little Bighorn, General Crook's troops were camped some distance away. They spent their time having a fishing contest, catching trout in Big Goose Creek, using artificial flies. On the same day that Generals Gibbon and Terry were rescuing survivors of the battle, Crooks' soldiers caught 146 trout. Later, some Indians showed up, and demonstrated how they caught trout. They constructed a weir and then rode downstream. They rode back up in the middle of the stream, thrashing the water with branches, driving the trout before them. The trout, trapped by the weir, were easy pickings. "That's how real men catch fish," the Indians told the soldiers.

SNOW IN THE VACANT lot in Arlington Heights.

It drifts onto I-5 at Dunsmuir, and disappears in the water in the Middle Fork of the Feather in a long pool above Laymans Resort.

It is surprisingly there when Paul and I leave the bar at Mt. Tomba and Paul stands in the drifting snow in short sleeves while I take his photograph.

Snow packed in the road above Alder Springs where the children slide in the ruts on an old Radio Flyer sled with steel runners, the same kind of sled we had in Elgin when

I was eight, coming out of the snow-covered cemetery at the top of the street.

Snow drifts on a cabin in the Sierras, one with a stove filled with crackling wood, the door open so we can see the flames from the bed; snow caps the river rocks. Snow powders the deck that faces the river.

Snow blowing sideways as the drift boat spins slowly, settling into a long run.

Snow swallowing sound, no bird song, no raucous jays, no cows, no wind.

Snow at Dodge Ridge when I was a teenager, wearing my waxed jeans. Someone had told me that waxing them would make them waterproof and I spent hours dripping candle wax onto them, rubbing it in until the fabric was stiff. It didn't work and I was wet and cold that first time on skis.

Snow on the ridges the day I poured Art's ashes in the Middle Fork and Nelson Creek, a spit of snow when I climbed out onto the old Nelson Point Bridge. The trees were shrouded in whirling white.

Snow in the prairie fields of Bureau County where my grandfather took my grandmother for a sleigh ride, pulled by a farm horse before they were married. She noted it in a diary she kept as a young woman, working as a farm girl for a neighboring farmer. "Oh, it was wonderful!" she wrote.

Snow, whiter than this page.

Snow falling outside the windows of the elementary school in Arlington Heights. I was in the fourth grade, and I walked to school, wearing galoshes and mittens and then the snow came again, soft flakes drifting, muting the two story red brick building, a squat fortress that was surrounded by bare trees. The wooden desks were bolted to the floor in rows, the lids could be lifted and there was an empty hole where an inkwell had been, stained around the edges. I was in a row next to the windows, tall double-hung windows that could be opened in the hot September days to let whatever breeze stirred through the classroom, but now they were closed and the snow drifted past, and I watched it until the teacher called my name, "Russell!" and I realized she had asked a question and once again, I had been what she called day dreaming. But I was remembering a story in *Real Tales for Real Dogs* by Albert Payson Terhune, about a dog that had struggled through the snow to carry a message across the battlefield. My head was filled with stories. It still is.

Snow when the geese came and a distant relative named Spratt took his shotgun and a sheet into the field to cover himself and his dog, waiting for the geese to circle the field.

Snow on the Saval ranch north of Elko, blowing across the dirt road, darkening the mountains to the north. Gance Creek will freeze and the Humboldt cutthroat trout will sink to the bottom, move like molasses, their metabolic rate slowing, eating zooplankton and insect larva from the muddy bottom of the beaver dams. They wait patiently for the Spring thaw.

It is the Dead of Winter. It is a phrase that comes from the Old English, *motionless, still,* but the trout continue to move, undulate slowly, as they have done for twenty thousand years.

MAYFLIES emerging, caught in the surface of the water, trout rising, the hex hatch just at dark, loons and bats and the black surface of the lake and the *plouf!* of trout sipping at the surface, cold water against legs. And the long cast. More of them, rising from the deep to hatch at the place that is half water and half air, spinning up into the night, wings unfolding, emerging *Hexegenia ephemereoptera*, 300 million years old rising from waters in Mississippi and California and Pennsylvania, transparent in the yellow street lights in June. A trout rises in the blackness, suddenly breaking the surface, and we call to each other across the water and wait for the invisible certainty.

RED COLUMNS OF LIGHT rise on the brown brick building to the north and east of the hotel. They are rose-colored streaks that highlight the corners and edges. Bright arc lights beam from a bridge over the Sacramento River and fourteen stories below the traffic is steady, white headlights and red taillights. A theater sign flashes red and blue and yellow and the sky is dark, a black layer of cloud below the dull blue of the night sky.

When I was a boy I came through Sacramento on a train named The Overland Limited, pulled by a great Malley steam engine. The engine was designed by Anatole Mallet, and had sixteen giant driving wheels, another eight smaller wheels, and the locomotive was articulated so that on sharp curves the boiler stuck out to one side, the most powerful steam engine in the world. When, as a teenager, I worked at *Feather River Camp*, I could hear the Malleys coming up canyon, pulling a hundred freight cars, the heavy beat of the engine driving and then silence when it went into a tunnel, a sudden louder chant when it came out, and forty-five minutes later it came past camp, driving so powerfully that the ground shook.

Trout in the deep pools on Spanish Creek below the camp stopped rising after the train passed and we waited on the bank among the green elephant ears until they began to dimple the surface again.

And now I look from the hotel window out toward the river and remember the long Pullman cars, the dark green corridors of curtains during the night, the swaying of the cars as we slept and the chime of the black porter as he announced that the dining car was open.

In the morning the rain begins, the streets shine and just west of Sacramento in a field as green as the felt on a pool table, four egrets rise, white slashes in the mist. On highway 37 two more row across the sky, their necks bent in an S, their wings a measured beat against the windshield wipers. They are an erotic bird, stalkers that move silently, patiently graceful, never in flocks like screaming crows or whirling black birds, erect, their long necks a stroke from an artist's brush, single strokes here and there in the flooded rice fields or soft marshes.

I FIRST CLIMBED the Sutter Buttes, also known as the Marysville Buttes, when I was a teenager. The Buttes rise out of the upper Sacramento Valley, reputed to be the world's smallest mountain chain. A high school friend who was into climbing long before it became a popular sport, invited me to join him and two friends in a climb of the east slope of the steepest butte. Roped together, we spent four hot, exhausting hours working our way up, dodging poison oak, grasping crumbling rocks, and came out on top, sweating and dirty, to be greeted by a group of Catholic school girls and a nun in full habit. They had come up the easy incline on the west side of the butte. I remember one of the girls: her white blouse and plaid school skirt, dark haired, Hispanic and quite beautiful.

The trapper and explorer Jedediah Smith came to the Buttes in 1828 to escape the flooding Sacramento River. The water, he claimed, became a sea that stretched from the Sierra foothills to the Coastal Range. He was not greeted by a beautiful schoolgirl. He found elk, deer, bear, coyotes and rattlesnakes, all fleeing the rising water. Now, the Big Oro

Dam, Bullards Bar and Shasta Dam control the spring flood. The Buttes rise out of the valley near the wetlands that harbor hundreds of thousands of ducks and geese every year. They must have darkened the sky in Smith's time. On fall days when the rice farmers burn the stubble in the fields, the Buttes are smoky outlines. That school girl, if she is still alive, would be in her late seventies. I wonder if she remembers the four teenage boys who came over the crest of South Butte.

THEY USED TO BURN the rice stubble every fall in the Central Valley, long lines of flame, thick smoke rising. Sunsets were brilliant and the air smelled of burning grass. When I saw those long lines of flame I thought of the prairie fires that the early sod busters faced, shoulder high grass on fire sweeping across the horizon as far as they could see. Prairie fires burned hay, feed, barns, animals, houses, and whole towns. They moved as fast as the wind. They no longer burn the stubble in the rice fields, and prairie fires are rare. The long grasses of the prairie have disappeared along with the millions of bison. In California's Central Valley geese and ducks gather to pick at the grains left by the rice harvesters. The air is clear and the Coast Range outline is sharp.

There is something about fires in the Fall. When I was a boy in Illinois leaves were raked into a pile at the curb and set alight. Men stood with rakes, pulling the leaves into the flame until all that was left was ash. The ash washed away with the first rain. I do not know where it went.

Fall marked Guy Fawkes night in England. The children of Shillingstone Primary School heaped things in a pile on the playing field: old chairs, broken boxes, cast off clothes dressed on an effigy of Guy Fawkes. Villagers dropped off old furniture, a discarded door, a pile of branches from a fallen tree. The pile grew. And on Monday night, November fifth, when it became dark and the villagers had gathered in a circle, John Plumpton, the headmaster of the school doused the edge with petrol and threw a match and it erupted. The bonfire grew, throwing sparks into the night air and boys threw firecrackers into the flames.

Two weeks ago flames erupted near Pulga in the Feather River Canyon and raced over the ridges to consume the towns of Paradise and Magalia. People fled for their lives, many of them perishing in the flames, and the black and red sky was visible from Chico, miles away in that valley where the rice fields once burned. The smoke drifted down the Central Valley and blanketed the San Francisco Bay Area, forcing people to wear masks. Pictures of people in Beijing wearing similar masks were common.

The Paradise fire was not a Guy Fawkes fire. This was a fire that consumed people's homes, their belongings, their personal history and for some of them, their lives. This was a fire that left automobiles as burned out hulks, whole neighborhoods nothing but ash. It has been almost fifty years since I drove down the Central Valley with those rice fields burning.

ON READING THE WORDS Chesil Beach. For my birthday I was given a copy of Ian McEwan's new novel, *On Chesil Beach*. There is a photograph of Chesil Beach on the cover. The words Chesil Beach bring back an image. My wife, Eleanor, and three children and I stood on that English beach on a windy November day thirty-five years ago, and the shelf of stones ran down into the water where the waves rushed over them with a continuous white noise. There was no sand. Only stones. All of the stones where we stood were uniform, about the size of marbles. Two hundred yards south of us they were the size of beans. But trudging through the soft dunes of stones to the north, they grew bigger. Miles up the beach they were said to be the size of cricket balls. Locals said they could tell where they were on the beach by the size of the stones. Smugglers in the old days, they said, came onto the beach in the dark, and the size of the stones told them where they had landed. Eleanor, our three children and I, stretched out our arms, leaning into the fierce wind off the English Channel, our jackets unzipped, as if we had wings and our four-year-old son, Graham, was lifted off his feet by the wind, falling back into the stones.

All of that day is inside my head. Parts of it are inside the heads of my wife and children, but they will, of course, remember it differently than I do. And when I think of the soft bank of stones and my feet slipping in them, sliding toward the sea, I think of English Bar, a great bank of stones on the Middle Fork of California's Feather River. It was years ago, and the man I was fishing with was a young man who grew old and is now dead. We stepped off the edge of the bank of stones and they were like ball bearings under our feet and we descended like drunks to the edge of the river, sliding into the cold water, holding our fly rods high so that they wouldn't bang against the rocks and break.

The words *Chesil Beach* will trigger things in my head that aren't in Eleanor's head, even though she was there on that beach with me. Perhaps the word beach will resurrect the beach in Chicago on the edge of Wacker Drive when she was in her twenties.

The photograph on the cover of McEwan's book shows a long strand of darkness under a solitary figure. There is no way to know that it is made of tiny stones. No wind blows across the cover of the book.

So there are the two words: *Chesil* and *Beach.* My students will think of summers and getting a tan and sneaking off to find a beer hidden in a cooler in the grass and they will not see the desolate stretch of stones nor hear the rush of water polishing them or lean into the wind and imagine that they are flying. Nor will they find themselves sliding down a wall of stones with a dead man who has suddenly come to life.

I HAVE BEEN READING an Icelandic author, Arnaldur, and find his writing compelling. Iceland has few people and they live in an unforgiving geography and climate. These are police procedural novels, and the central character must deal with violent crime, and often the arctic weather plays a part. Sometimes he reflects on events that happened in his childhood and this is one of those reflections:

He enjoyed traveling alone; the gradual sensation of being overwhelmed by the profound solitude of his childhood haunts, surrounded by places and incidents from a past that was still vivid to him, that filled him with nostalgia. He knew it only existed in his memory. When he was gone there would be nothing left. When he was gone it would be as if none of it had ever existed.

I might have written that. It's certainly a theme that I have visited from time to time.

Earlier in this collection of thoughts, I wrote about my son-in-law Dave and Art Morris. Both of them are dead and what I have left are memories and a few photographs. I wrote about being at Yellow Creek with Art:

That evening the coyotes began to talk across the little valley, barking from one side, another pack responding from the other. Cattle came down to the creek, their hooves slurping in the mud, and we lit a fire and drank a scotch. The isolation that evening was complete. The silence was immense. When I look at the photographs of Dave and Art I am reminded of that isolation. It is as if there is a hole in my memory, a classroom blackboard wiped clean, jackets that no longer have a hook to hang them on. Take the fucking picture, Art probably said. I took it.

Arnaldur's character tells us about being caught in a blizzard with his father and his younger brother, and the two of them becoming separated from the father. He loses his grip on his brother's hand, and the brother is lost in the blizzard, his body never recovered. I wrote about taking my younger brother, Paul, on a journey in the late fall. We were the same ages as Andular's characters, ten and seven. We found ourselves overtaken by darkness and freezing cold. We were not caught in a blizzard, nor did either of us come to harm. I, too, held my brother's hand as we trudged through abandoned corn fields, the freezing mud clinging to our shoes, and my relief when we were discovered by a policeman who had been looking for us, and our eventual return home. But Andular's character touches something within me and his reflection on the memories of childhood is so close it might easily be my own.

I WAKE AT THREE o'clock in the morning. I am wide awake. I turn on the lamp above my head and reach for my reading glasses that lie on the bed beside me. Then I open the book that lies there also. This morning it is a book by Henning Mankell, a mystery, and I read until five thirty. It crosses my mind that Henning Mankel is now dead.

I read his final book, *Quicksand, What It Means to Be a Human Being*, written after he knew that he was dying. He wrote in an early chapter, *"I noticed that my memory often transported me back to my childhood. But it wasn't long before I realized that my memory was trying to help me to understand, to create a starting point that would enable me to cope with the potentially fatal catastrophe with which I had been stricken."* The starting point he selects is when he is nine years old, on his way to school.

In this book, *Ghost Trout,* I, too, selected a point similar to that one. I was nine years old at school in Arlington Heights, Illinois, and the snow was swirling past the tall double-hung windows of the old classroom and I found myself daydreaming that I was outside in that snow.

My early morning reading has become a habit and I am wondering if it is in response to my memory of Fred Lakosky, who went to sleep and did not wake up. Perhaps if I read until it is time to rise, I will cheat the twin brother of sleep.

But, of course, I could just as easily have a heart attack while I am turning to chapter twenty-three.

It is no longer light at five-thirty. It is still dark out. Another summer is slipping away. I must paint the white trim on the front windows, stain the trim on the kitchen window, secure the flashing on the greenhouse before the rains come. Those are small projects that assume I will be here when the rains come, and I will be pleased that I have waterproofed the vulnerable places in my house. I have done this for more than fifty years. Whoever buys this house when I am gone will, no doubt, drop its roof and walls, strip it back to the foundation and another house will rise, just as his one did, with tighter doors and floors that do not squeak, wide windows that frame a view of Mt. Tamalpais.

Three o'clock turns to four and then to five and Mankell's characters wander though Sweden, a country I have never visited, except through his words. For two hours this morning, I have experienced the snow and wind of Sweden, not unlike the snow of my childhood, nine years old, looking out the window of the Arlington Heights Elementary School, watching the flakes drifting past.

GARY TEPLY, my neighbor of forty years, has thirty days left. Maybe less. He is, like the river in late summer, slowing, the eddies curling among the rocks, and there will be no winter storm that will fill him, make him spill over into another year.

This morning I sat across from him, and he asked me to buy him some cigarettes. What difference does it make? The cancer is creeping down his neck, will shut off his voice, make it hard for him to eat.

I offer him a scotch. He has bought a bottle of Johnnie Walker Black Label for me as thanks for cutting wood, and re-hanging his door to the deck and being a friend. "Not necessary," I say, but it's scotch I cannot afford, and it is a gesture that is generous and kind; I open the bottle, pour him a drink and say, "Here's to something," but I cannot think of what to say.

Here's to endings. The end of the football game at Piedmont High School when I was fourteen, we all climbed the hill to the church where there was a dance and I waited, palms sweating, for some girl to approach, and later I went out onto the wet street where a streetcar waited, its lights reflecting off the pavement.

The end of my long-time fishing partner, Art Morris, when he said, from his hospital bed, "Fuck this! Fuck this!" and I had no answer for that, either.

The end of my father, lying in a bed on the opposite side of the glass window in the isolation ward, tuberculosis filling his lungs.

The end of school each June, the classroom suddenly empty and the jostle of teenage voices and bodies gone.

The end of a weekend of fishing, climbing the canyon wall to sit on the edge of the gravel road, smoking a cigarette, the afternoon light fading.

The end of the evening at Bushrod Center in North Oakland's black neighborhood, turning out the lights in the gym, waiting for the last basketball players to leave, going out into the night on Grove Street and finding my car. I was the only white face in that gym, and I learned to speak another language, and at the end of the day I was suddenly no longer part of their world.

The end of my older brother, a sudden clutching in his chest and he, too, was no longer there.

My son-in-law Dave, stricken with cancer, sitting in his garage, looking at his workman's hands, knowing that they would no longer work.

Now I sit across the room from Gary and realize that his end is nearing. And that he knows it, and I wonder what goes through his mind as he contemplates the finish of his life.

What was it T.S. Eliot said in the *Four Quartets*? "In the beginning is my end."

Now comes the end for Gary. I climb his stone path and cut blocks of wood on the chop saw, pile them up so he can stoke his wood stove. Mario, his neighbor, says it's like having a continuous election of the Pope next door, grey smoke rising every morning. Mario is a trumpeter with an international reputation. The long solo at the beginning of *The Godfather* is Mario, and in the afternoon we can hear him practicing scales, still polishing his craft.

I find myself writing about Gary, fitting the pieces of the puzzle together, and it is like that thousand piece puzzle my older brother and I completed one summer, standing on opposite sides of the table, silent in the early morning, searching for the tiny bit of blue sky or ocean. Now I need to find the pieces that are Gary, who stood across the street in front of the mailboxes, and we talked and cars that came up the hill slowed, the drivers waving at us.

A coyote came up the steps at Gary Teply's house, entered the greenhouse and stood, looking at Gary through the open door of the kitchen. The house is surrounded by trees. Years ago he brought saplings and tiny sprouts from the top of the ridge and now they blot out the sky, bend into each other. Ivy climbs the trunks, a stone path winds to the street. It was not a dog. It was a coyote. No one else has had a coyote look into their kitchen. Only Gary, who reclined in a chair, his bare feet on a footstool, wearing sweatpants, his thin legs covered by a blanket. His face was drawn and his voice soft. The coyote came up the stairs into the greenhouse, looked through the open kitchen door at Gary, turned and went back down the stairs. No words were exchanged.

I brought Gary his morning newspapers, found his glasses for him, went out into the back patio to cut several pieces of wood on the chop saw for his stove. Last week a surgeon opened his skull, took out pieces of a tumor attached to his brain. Light floods in the windows behind him. Gary made those windows, opening his house to the southern sun. The door to the greenhouse is open but there is no coyote. The greenhouse roof is made of shower doors he scavenged at the old dump on the edge of the bay. Somehow it is appropriate. Gary's great grandmother lived in a sod house on the frontier of Nebraska.

Orchids grow in his greenhouse. One night he came across the street to tell us his night-blooming orchid was about to open. That night it flowered, sending out a powerful scent. A night blooming orchid.

A great blue heron came down into his yard, threading its way among the trees to stab the fish in his ponds. A raccoon that lived under his house died among the pipes of his bathroom. Wild turkeys roosted on the ridge of his roof. A deer gave birth in the bushes under his deck. A coyote brought its dog-shape up his steps as if invited. Gary's house is imprinted with his signature: a room with a parquet floor made of the ends of two by fours, sanded for months, the cracks filled with linseed oil and sawdust; a pine floor of shelving that was on special at the lumber yard, glowing yellow in the afternoon light; shingles on the ceilings, cabinet doors with stucco infused with straw, burnished to a shine; a bathroom with an oak tree leaning into it. Whoever buys that house will either level it, or spend a fortune putting it on a foundation. An expensive new house will rise and no raccoon will take up residence under it. And there will not be a night-blooming orchid sending its powerful scent into the ragged oaks and pines. I will no longer cross the street in search of a tool. No great blue heron will descend among the pines and oaks to find a goldfish in a tiny pond.

And no coyote will come up the steps again.

This morning the crows were spiraling down into the trees across the canyon as I came up the driveway to find the newspapers. There was a single light burning in Gary's empty basement. I went up to turn it off and found that it was a light that I had never seen burning before. There seemed to be no switch and I tried to trace the wiring, but it disappeared among the floor joists into a rat's nest of wires. Somewhere in the house someone had thrown a switch and the light had gone on. And only Gary would know where that switch was. But Gary was gone, and the light burned all night, a yellow glow among the trees. They will have to demolish the house to extinguish that light.

CHRIS STREMPEK drove the first four hours up through the Sierras, dropping into the alkali flats of Nevada. Ellen drove the next four hours, Interstate 80 unwinding beneath us, the truck at a steady eighty miles an hour. The highway was a monotonous ribbon that led us past the Carson Sink, the

Cortez Mountains, the Humboldt Range, the Sheep Creek Range, the Piñon Range, Lovelock. Winnemucca and Battle Mountain came and went and we detoured through Carlin where I spent twenty-four hours as a teenager, discovering that I wasn't strong enough to last at a job in the Pacific Fruit Express icing station. The icing station had long since burned to the ground, and the bar where I asked midnight directions was boarded up, holes in the windows, weeds at the door.

And then we were in Elko, the neon lights glowing, the streets hot, and we had a scotch, swam in the motel pool, and ate a huge dinner in a Basque restaurant. At the bar in the Star Hotel, the tiny woman bartender made Picon punches for the three of us. We touched glasses and said, "Here's to the Humboldt cutt tomorrow."

An old rancher in a white Stetson looked at Chris and said, "I hate to break your heart, son, but this has been the driest summer in forty years. You may find your creek is dust and rocks."

We left Elko at eight the following morning under a cloudless sky, driving north on the two-lane highway that rose toward Boise. An hour later we found the turnoff to Saval Ranch. The Independence Mountains were in front of us, a plume of dust billowing behind the truck. The slopes were brown and bare, rising out of the sagebrush flats. A few cattle appeared and then the green patch that marked the ranch in the far distance. The ranch grew, cottonwood trees shading a low building, several barns and outbuildings, corrals, and beyond, the intense green of what had to be Gance Creek. We stopped at a locked gate. A yellow sign announced

POSTED NO HUNTING FISHING TRESPASSING
WITHOUT WRITTEN PERMISSION.

Three small dogs rushed, growling and barking frantically. A woman appeared outside the distant ranch house, walking the long curving road toward us. The dogs retreated, gathered about her legs, and the silence was complete. When she was close enough to speak, we could see that she was young, quite beautiful, wearing a plaid shirt and a denim skirt that brushed her ankles.

We asked about Gance Creek and the Humboldt cutt; she laughed, said her husband might know, but she had no idea where there might be trout in this barren landscape. She pointed up the canyon that rose above the ranch house, and told us that a road went farther up to a campground, and perhaps there was a creek there.

I thanked her, paused, looked up at the naked mountains. "Lots of solitude," I said. She smiled again.

"I like it," she said. She turned. "Come on girls," and the dogs gathered around her.

The dirt road narrowed, wide enough only for the truck, sagebrush and chaparral brushing the fenders. Around a corner two steers stared at our approach, slowly moving off to join others on the now steep hillside. Sage grouse ran in the dusty track and we slowed to a crawl.

Eventually we came to a fork where the road dipped back down toward a green mass of willows and cottonwoods. We stopped and when Chris and I approached the impenetrable green. He said, "I hear water." And yes, there was a tiny creek, not two feet wide, underneath the tangle.

We drove back down the spur road and parked. The willows, aspens and cottonwoods were so thick that it was difficult to find the stream. Behnke writes that *phreatophytes* are plants whose roots extend downward toward the water table. This riparian vegetation, transpiring huge amounts of water, drains the creek, crowding together in walls of interlaced branches, making it the most difficult fishing imaginable. Only here and there were narrow tunnels created by cattle forcing their way through. Dried cow flops were everywhere, and when we found a spot on the creek that had a few yards of open bank, the edge was thick mud, turned to mush by cattle hooves. The combination of thick vegetation, grazing damage, and a series of beaver dams, meant that the water was warmer and filled with nutrients that would peril any other trout. But the Humboldt cutt had evolved over thousands of years, able to survive in water that approached eighty degrees, sometimes in ponds that bloomed with algae and were so toxic with alkali that other fish bellied-up.

Somewhere in the impenetrable thicket the creek flowed. It did not bubble or talk like other small creeks I have known. It whispered and when it met a beaver dam it pooled in a grey cloud, so that a trout might only become an indistinct shadow if it moved.

Among the willows were other clutching shrubs, some of them armored with thorns that tore at my shirt and Levis.

I found myself trapped, unsure how I had entered the maze, cursing the willows and the fucking thorns, trying to extricate myself, my fly rod tangled among the branches, knowing I could not reach the water, sweating and finally fighting my way up into the sagebrush.

Ellen caught the first Humboldt cutthroat trout. She said it was bright orange and green, and I remembered Prosek's watercolor, a vivid slash of gold and pale green. The trout Chris caught was like Joseph Tomelleri's painting in Behnke's book, big spots, greenish with a lateral rose ribbon on its flank. Later, I stood on the muddy bank and, through the tangle of willows, watched Ellen's rod bend in an arc as a cutthroat danced across the dark water.

So, six years after I started my search, I saw this elusive

creature, deep in a labyrinth of brush and thorns, the water murky, just as Behnke had written.

I had found the tiny Humboldt cutthroat trout and Willa Cather was right. We tell the same two or three stories over and over. Back in Elko we had a scotch and felt the cool night air descending. We walked the streets, photographing the neon signs that shouted CASINO! and GIRLS! and MOTEL! and DANCING! The barren mountains and the spider web of Gance Creek seemed a thousand miles away.

FULL MOON OVER THE GREAT BASIN. The sage is milky and indistinct. Walk the dirt road that leads to the dark mountains, and the Columbia plateau to the north. Somewhere there are night creatures, relatives of dogs and cats, and things that crawl: bobcats and coyotes and snakes. Ground birds nest in the chaparral, alert in their sleep and the moon is a disc in the night sky. Cattle are asleep, standing, heads down, motionless, invisible. The day was hot, heat shimmering on the road ahead, mirage lakes appeared and we drove into them and they were gone. At night the temperature plummeted, cold enough for sweaters.

The same moon rises over the desert in Morocco and lights the white rapids on the North Fork of the Yuba. The Sierra Buttes are alight, muted, looming above us.

In the Central Valley egrets tuck their heads into their shoulders, becoming white stumps at the edge of the rice fields. The rice glows in the moonlight, pale green, still. The afternoon wind has died, as if it sank into the wet fields. It is the breath of the valley, an exhalation that is like a breathing through silk, touching your face and your body and lifting the birds that float above the rice fields.

The wind rises in the canyons, sweeping up from the valley as the heat rises, stirring the surface of the water behind the dams, and the generator at Bucks Creek runs full, the water coming out of the powerhouse in a great rush of white spume. Now there is only the whine of the turbines and the white disc pasted in the black opening above the canyon.

In the high desert of Nevada we feel the earth moving beneath that moon, turning on its axis, the Sierras rising behind us until, at first light, the moon becomes a pale circle pasted on the grey sky. False dawn outlines the Rubies.

The bats come out at dusk, a wind of black rising from under the bridges. Every evening, when the car lights go on, they suddenly appear, a cloud that dissipates, feasting on the insects that fill the humid air.

The folds of the mountain darken, turn from green to blue; the stillness of the evening, like the desert, only the birds and now the wind rising up canyon.

This morning, at five, I heard the coyotes, their shrill yips and howls punctuating the stillness. In the silent kitchen, the refrigerator hums.

Summer is here, the rivers are white and the heat rises all afternoon, wilting only when the sun drops below the ridge. The rivers run to the sea and I stand in the cold water, the current pulling at my calves and there is change all around me: trees growing green, an egret rowing upstream into the forest, and I am, each instant, older, changed, like an old dog that waits by the door, half barks at a stranger.

I pour myself a scotch, watch the sun go off the mountain, the evening shadows deepen, I remember the bark of sea lions beyond the breakers.

AUTUMN RAIN, wet leaves flattened against rocks like gold paper, the fall of the year, October and November, months when we hold each other for warmth; there is a sadness in the air, a slipping-away of summer's quickness, a slowing. Mist envelops the canyon, rain dapples the surface of the creek.

We are wet, the grass is wet, a jay hunches above us, feathers wet, eye cocked at us, grey skies, grey clouds, grey rocks, color dissolves in the rain, autumn, the last part of someone's life, the autumn years, a polite way of marking closeness to the end. The Irish word is *fogamon,* under-winter. Lithuanians say *ruduo,* reddish, and the leaves on Greenhorn Creek turn red and yellow and gold above the ancient car bodies stacked along the bank, put there by some farmer in the '30's to control erosion, and now big trout lurk behind the long-ago shattered windshields, fin slowly where transmissions have rusted, and the rain comes again, harder, slanting across the meadow.

October light, soft, no longer the hard light of July, and there is no common word for *autumn* among the Europeans.

But this is not Europe. The water from the spring at Mt. Tomba bubbles from the pipe and there is ice in the morning and the trees at Sloat, where there was a mill, are gold. At dusk the grass crunches underfoot.

We will go back to the cabin and drink scotch and there will be braised rabbit and the rain will turn to snow and autumn will dissolve into winter.

IT WAS A DANCE STUDIO in Oakland. 1945 or '46. At night. Juanita Miller leaped onto the table, scarves floating around her as if she were Isadora Duncan. But she was, I thought, an old woman. I was astounded. Juanita Miller, daughter of the California poet, Joaquin Miller.

Every year she produced a melodrama that was performed on an outdoor stage in the Oakland hills in the park named after her father. It was an amateurish script with bad guys and good guys, a sheriff and a posse and Juanita Miller. My great uncle Howard was the sheriff. We went to the rehearsals in the park and I was one of the sheriff's deputies, no doubt because my uncle Howard was cast as the sheriff. I remember almost nothing of it except the rehearsal in a dance studio in Oakland, and Juanita Miller doing the dance that she would do in the play. She would be kidnapped and the sheriff and his posse of deputies would come to her rescue and somewhere in there she would do her Isadora Duncan imitation. The dance seemed to have nothing to do with the plot of the play. She had to be old at that point. At least it seemed to me that she was an old woman, but to a ten year old she could very well have been in her sixties.

It was a simple time, a time when families went off to a park in the hills on a Saturday evening to watch a melodrama where the audience booed the villains, and cheered when the sheriff and his posse showed up. I carried a cap pistol and wore a flannel shirt and a straw hat, and charged onto the stage with the others when uncle Howard yelled, "Come on boys! Let's get 'em!" It was a warm summer night in Joaquin Miller Park where we acted out the drama on a wooden stage facing a small amphitheater set into a hillside, redwoods towering above us. A year before that I had been a nine-year old in Illinois, where I went to elementary school in a two-story brick building in a small town that would, over the years, grow to become a suburb of Chicago. Suddenly I had been dropped into an exotic world where old ladies danced on tables and the night sky was blacked out by trees taller than any I could have imagined. Juanita Miller danced, scarves floating about her, a vibrant woman who did not resemble any woman that I had ever seen.

Why am I remembering this now? Remembering that

night in Oakland in a cramped room with scarred hardwood floors and a table where an old woman leaped and stretched, filmy scarves wrapped around her body, her arms thrust into the air above us.

She was eccentric, as had been her father. He lived in a tiny cabin in what later became the park named after him. His poem, "Columbus," was memorized by nearly every schoolchild in America. "Sail on! Sail on! the Captain said."

When I found myself part of the cast of that Old West melodrama, I did not know who Joaquin Miller was. I only knew that the woman who rushed about giving directions and who was, obviously, the star of the show, was the daughter of a famous poet. Ambrose Bierce said he was "the greatest liar this country ever produced. He cannot or will not ever tell the truth."

I think my memory of Juanita Miller is the truth. I'm not sure any more what the truth is. I remember events that my brother, Paul, says are inaccurate. What he means is that I am remembering an event that did not happen, or happened in an entirely different way. Did Juanita Miller dance on that table? She must have. How could I invent that moment?

When I write a story, I find myself caught up in the characters, and they begin to resemble the truth, as if they are real people and all I have to do is remember what it was they said, what they did and how they did it. I know that there are moments in their lives that are, in fact, moments from my life. At three o'clock in the morning there are movies that play in my head, a screen that recreates scenes from my past, although sometimes they are only partly from my past and partly from what I might have wished in my past. I have difficulty separating the two. I am not sure I want to.

So, early in the morning while I lay in a hospital bed in San Francisco, Juanita Miller appeared, her scarves floating mysteriously about her, and I was disembodied, watching the ten-year-old who watched her. And then the screen shifted and I was in another place, watching someone else. Outside, in the hall, a monitor steadily beeped, and to my right was the pulsating rhythm of the saline drip and the faint echoes of traffic on Geary Boulevard five stories below. On the opposite wall were six pinpoints of light: two were an electric blue, three were yellow, and below that was one red light that blinked on and off. They were like a constellation in a night sky and I tried to connect them, make a shape like the ones in a school child's book on the heavens, but they refused to outline anything.

Juanita Miller had danced off to another room.

THE TRAIN WEST. In the spring of 1945 my father took the test given annually to school teachers for tuberculosis and to his chagrin, he tested positive. It meant that our lives would be turned upside down. He would go off to a sanitarium in New Mexico, the rented house would be emptied, and my mother would put us three boys, herself and great aunt Blanche on a train going west. Aunt Blanche was the sister of the woman whose house we would live in for the next five years. The train was filled with soldiers and sailors headed toward the Pacific war. Years later a cousin told us that there had been talk of splitting us three boys up, sending us off to the homes of uncles or cousins, but my mother was adamant and her mother's sister and husband who lived in California and were childless, took us in.

It was a Pullman train, cars that changed from rows of seats to a long corridor with heavy green curtains on either side at night, masking the berths that came down out of the ceiling and folded up out of the seats. I remember the men's room where a black porter shined shoes and soldiers stripped to the waist to shave and wash themselves. Paul and I slept together in a lower berth, my mother and Aunt Blanche in the berth above us. My older brother Ronald must have had his own berth. I stood on the steps of the car in Green River, Wyoming while they added an engine for the climb over the Rockies, steam coming from beneath the train while Paul took my picture with my Box Brownie camera. My father was gone. Somewhere in New Mexico. There had been no talk of him going and suddenly he wasn't there. I'm sure he said goodbye to us but there were no tearful farewells in our family. We were moving again, this time to someplace exotic near an ocean. We would cross two mountain chains and for the rest of my life I would be tied to the mountains and the sea.

My father went off to a sanitarium in the mountains of New Mexico. In those days, just about the only "cure" for TB was bed rest. There were other things they did, opening up the chest and collapsing a lung, patent medicines, but for the most part, the patient was told to stay still, read only books that were unexciting, walk about as little as possible. Their beds were open to the air, and in the mountains of New Mexico the night time temperatures dropped below freezing. It wasn't long before he was in another sanitarium on the outskirts of San Jose. Once again, the move wasn't talked about. Years later I was told that he wrote to my mother from the sanitarium in New Mexico and said that he was in a colony of men, living on the side of a mountain, waiting to die. The primary treatment consisted of "heliotherapy," which meant lying on slatted beds on the hillside in the sun, no matter what the temperature, as if breathing high-altitude air would somehow flush the tuberculosis from his lungs. And now he was in a cottage near San Jose with three other men, the walls folded up on all four sides like wings, and I could talk to him through the screened wall. I do not remember what we talked about. His disease was a mystery. Someone, somewhere, a doctor perhaps, would solve that mystery. I was ten.

I DO NOT REMEMBER my father much. Sometimes he was away, as he was when we lived in Elgin. By the time I was ten I should have formed memories of who he was, things that he said, a place in the house, but he remained a shadow and would remain so until he came back from the last sanitarium, his tuberculosis arrested. Even then, he remained someone who was only partially formed. He was a slight man by that time, perhaps a hundred and thirty pounds, not particularly tall, and only once did I see his naked chest. It was cadaverous, shrunken, and I knew when I saw it why he was always dressed in his white shirt. He had a thin face, and the glass eye gave him a look that was intense although, of course, since I didn't recognize it as an inert piece of glass, I assumed that there was a look that was more intense than perhaps it was. It was hard to reconcile his image with the yellowed newspaper clippings of him as a high school athlete.

My father was a meticulous man. His handwriting was small, neat, the letters perfectly formed, unlike my handwriting that looks, as one friend said, like a schoolboy's barely legible scrawl. He was a draftsman for a shipyard in a time when draftsmen used pencils and pens that were filled with ink, had to make perfect circles and intersections, and I remember blueprints, big sheets with white lines that showed studs and walls and joists and arrows with tiny numbers that outlined dimensions. He kept meticulous records of the family's expenses once he returned from the last sanitarium. He was, in a time when it was not usual, a house husband. My mother went off each morning to San Francisco to work. He kept the house organized, went to parent conferences at school for Paul, who was the wild one. Among things my mother left behind was a tablet with the monthly expenses, the numbers in columns that looked as if they had been printed by a machine. Ten cents for a postal stamp. Everything was carefully entered. He learned to cook dinner, spaghetti or fried chicken or casseroles that were heavy with tuna and canned mushroom soup. I do not remember him losing his temper. Had his enforced idleness in the sanitariums crushed his spirit or had he always been such a quiet, self-controlled man? No, my mother said when I was in my forties. Once, she said, he carried his keys attached to a heavy machine nut, waiting to be fired unfairly from a job. He planned, she said, to hurl the nut and the keys through the glass door of the owner's office. I could not imagine him doing that. I only know that he never raised his voice. Somehow, I imagine that before he went off to the magic mountain, he was different.

There is a photograph of the family after my grandmother Bickford died, taken outdoors in Wyanet. On the left is my Aunt Laura, my mother's sister; stocky Grandpa Bickford, coatless, in suspenders, the only one sitting, with Paul as a baby on his lap—it must have been a Sunday, he wears a tie; Ronald, probably ten years old, wears long trousers and a striped short-sleeved shirt. He is as tall as my mother's shoulders; next is my mother, then me in a little white sleeveless outfit with short pants. Next to me is my father, slacks, white shirt, the outline of his cigarette pack in his pocket. No one touches anyone else except Aunt Laura, who has her hand upon my grandfather's sleeve. There is a space between all of us, except for Ronald, who stands in front of my mother, but she does not reach out to touch him. The spaces would continue for the rest of our lives. My children's families gather with their arms around each other, pulling their bodies together. In this family we kept our bodies to ourselves; there is no hand on the shoulder of a child or an arm around someone.

Aunt Laura was different from her sister. She worked in Chicago, could drink and swear and unlike my modest mother, wore a dress that was sleeveless and cut low enough to show the plane of her chest and a faint décolletage. When we were teenagers, living in Aunt Laura's house in Berkeley, she lived in a one-room apartment on the second floor. Paul and a junior high school classmate drank some of her scotch, and replaced what they drank with water. She took Paul aside and told him that she was aware of what he had done. "It's a sin to water good scotch," she said. "Don't ever do that again." She never told our parents.

I have a memory of a photograph of four girls posing on the running board of an open car in front of a roadhouse somewhere in Illinois. There were Aunt Laura, my mother, and their two cousins, Madge and Ordell. Only Aunt Laura was dressed in the flapper style of the thirties. The others wore big hats and dresses that covered themselves, despite what looked like a hot Illinois sun. But there is a picture of my mother with a sorority sister at the University of Illinois in which she wears a filmy dress that does not hide her slender shape. This was the girl my father fell in love with and there is a hint of someone who was more than a modest farm girl.

But the mother I remember was reserved. She was not a toucher. She spoke quietly. It was not shyness. It was reservation, as if she kept her emotions in check, always aware of what others would think of her. Her job with the Pacific Fruit Express was to keep track of where the damaged freight cars were, what railroad had them, what stage of repair they were in. She kept these records on index cards in boxes, a mind-numbing job for a woman with a university education. The men in her office were, for the most part, high school graduates. She was a woman working in a man's world. It must have rankled when they came to her for advice on how to solve a problem.

For some reason I became enamored of tugboats. I built a crude model of one at Uncle Howard's workbench in the basement. One Saturday, mother took Paul and me to San Francisco on the electric train that crossed the bay on the lower deck of the Bay Bridge. We walked the Embarcadero until we came to the offices of the Red Stack Tugboat Company. There, in the lobby, were glass cases with detailed models of the Red Stack tugs. She had, in her lunch hour, walked down Market Street from New Montgomery and then along the Embarcadero to search out those models. I was excited at the sight of them. I drew sketches on a piece of paper. It is now, when I remember that Saturday morning when I was eleven years old, that I realize her quiet dedication to us.

I have thought of my place in the family, sandwiched between two brothers. My older brother became a brilliant mathematician and wore three-piece suits, wing-tip shoes and a Homburg hat long after the rest of the workaday world had abandoned such garb. He was incredibly neat, and caused little trouble for my mother. My younger brother was less meticulous, but he became an engineer and as he grew older, he, too, began to carefully organize his life. I was the one in the middle. There had been another brother, older than me, who had died in infancy, Francis. Somehow the name fits a child who didn't survive his first year. Caught between those two, I spent my time lost in books, lived for the most part in a world of fiction, was often late for dinner, and in high school was thrown out of chemistry for lack of attention to important details. "If you had paid attention," the chemistry teacher said, "that would not have happened. You endangered us all."

Robert Penn Warren wrote in a poem titled, "Two Poems about Suddenly and a Rose,"

Suddenly, suddenly, everything
Happens, it seems.

Bob Feller pitched for the Cleveland Indians when he was seventeen years old. He threw a fastball a hundred miles an hour, but batters weren't sure where it would go.

They didn't crowd the plate and Leo Durocher, who faced Feller in his first game, turned to the umpire and said, "I feel like a duck in a shooting gallery." Suddenly, Feller was no longer a farm boy on a cornfield baseball diamond.

JFK waved to the Dallas onlookers and suddenly he slumped forward, his brain shattered by an assassin's bullet.

Suddenly, my daughter's husband, Dave, was diagnosed with cancer. Suddenly he was no longer the muscular man on a construction site; he sat in his garage and looked through the open door at the empty street and waited.

My oldest son was on his way to his teaching job, riding his motorcycle on an empty Central Valley highway when, suddenly, a farm truck pulled out in front of him and he was on the pavement, his hip shattered and his life changed.

Suddenly. From the Latin, *to approach stealthily.* It sneaks up on you.

Suddenly, I could no longer see the trout rising at the edge of the cove.

Suddenly I was no longer in chemistry. I hadn't planned it that way when the day started. It just happened.

AREQUIPPA. The photograph is eight by ten, glossy, and it shows a big room, open to the rafters, the left side filled with floor-to-ceiling windows. The tall windows are hinged at the middle, on pivot pins, so that they can be opened top and bottom at the same time. On the right wall are beds: iron bedsteads painted white, white sheets and pillows. Despite the openness of the room, there is darkness to it. A single woman sits in a straight-backed chair on the left side. She is slender, dressed in a simple shift, and perhaps there is another woman in one of the beds, although she might be turned away from the camera so that only the heaped sheet hints that there is a body under it. There is a chair at the end of each bed, and the room is orderly and simple to the point of deprivation. Sleep, rest, sleep and more rest. Tuberculosis. Young women from San Francisco came to my little town in the hills of Marin County where they hoped to recover. It was a desperate hope.

It was widespread. Many women. The bacillus was airborne, women stayed indoors, caring for children, cooking, cleaning, and they passed the disease to each other while the men went out into the open air to work. I talked to an old chemist named Samways in Dorset who said that when he was a boy, every woman and girl in his village had the consumption. They came to his father's apothecary for patent medicine, but there was no cure, only a steady decline, a quiet death heralded by racking coughs and an eventual cascade of bright blood hemorrhaging from the lungs.

In operas, divas lay in death throes, but here at Arequippa they walked slowly, lay in the sun, and made little ceramic pots that were sold to help pay for their care.

Now it's a Girl Scout retreat. That long room filled with the dust motes of a July afternoon where the women lay on their beds or sat in their chairs, forbidden to read anything that would race their minds, but contains girls who chatter and run about, filling the room with energy. In some sanitariums doctors with an experimental bent collapsed lungs, breaking ribs in the process and in others there were doses of strange mixtures, none of them worth the cost of the contents. They hung patients upside down, hoping to collapse part of their lungs. But Arequippa, patterned after Saranac Lake in New York, tried to arrest the disease through rest and minimal exercise. Only a single shower a week, food that was bland, conversation that was limited to a word or two.

The pottery flourished, time spent at spinning wheels, shaping the bowls and teapots, glazing them, not speaking but thinking of children left with relatives, waiting for the Sunday visits that were all too seldom. The summer days were hot, insects chorusing in the oak trees and below, in the town of Fairfax, the occasional sound of a car laboring up White's Hill toward the coast, or the rumbling single-car train waiting to return to Sausalito. Bark peeled in curlicues from the madrone trees, *los arboles rojos,* and the pines filled the air with the scent of turpentine.

Look again at the photograph: she sits, primly, waiting for the shutter to click. She is someone's mother, brought here hoping that she will live long enough to watch her children grow, see them bloom and now she waits, keeping her body still, willing the disease to go away. The windows are open. The hot July day filters in.

My father waited in a different sanitarium in New Mexico. A colony of men on the side of a mountain waiting to die, he said.

They named it *consumption.* It consumed its victims, silently eating the vitality of their lungs. But, unlike the soprano in the opera, it was a quiet death, the expulsion of a last breath and then silence. No applause. No rising for a curtain call. Only a straight-backed chair in a silent room with the whine of insects filling the afternoon air.

NELSON CREEK, mid-August. It was hot in the Feather River Canyon, at least a hundred degrees, the road shimmering, and still hot when we turned off above Quincy onto the La Porte road. It was early afternoon, and the hike down to Nelson Point was warm even though we were at 4,000 feet. The trail was powdery and the Middle Fork, when we reached it, was green and cool and running slowly. The water temperature was 72° but Nelson Creek, spilling into the slower water of the Middle Fork was more than fifteen degrees cooler. When I stepped into the water to wade across my feet were suddenly cold and it felt good. No waders that afternoon. Just wading boots and Levis and the cold wash of the clear water. Geoff was ahead of me and I fished slowly, working back and forth across the stream, pausing to strip out line, lay a fly in the race above a pool, careful not to spook the fish. At one long pool I watched while a half dozen trout worked below me and as soon as I moved—only one step— they spooked, darting upstream.

Long grass streams into the water along one rock ledge, green fronds that trailed the edge of the current, shading the overhang and I floated a fly carefully along the edge, hoping that the big brown that lived there would rise, but it was the heat of the afternoon and there was no hatch, only the still air.

I stopped to change leaders, change the fly. Take off the elk hair caddis and tie on a tiny winged ant, hoping that it would bring up something. But I didn't go back to the stream immediately. I waited, listening to the water, watching damsel flies dimple the surface, their iridescent blue bodies glinting in the sun.

The afternoon waned and shadow filled the canyon. I took tiny trout and released them and then the wind came up, riffling the water, making it difficult to cast. I was growing tired now.

When I was twenty or thirty I could fish until it was black, but now I felt it in my legs, the jarring over rocks, the thin air, the afternoon heat, the surge of water when I waded across the stream and I turned back, started downstream, fishing the same pools I fished on the way up. Along one ledge I floated the fly carefully, casting from thirty feet downstream, crouching, almost on my knees and there was a miniature explosion of water and the trout took line and when I brought it to the edge it was as bright as new chrome.

Now I was at the foot of the trail and I waited for Geoff, watching the water darken, knowing that he would fish until the light failed, remembering how I used to fish on Spanish Creek until it was dark, climb out onto the railroad tracks and come back, stumbling along the ties into the first tunnel where it was so black that if I held my hand in front of my face I only knew it was there by blowing on it.

When Geoff appeared over the gravel bar at the bend above me it was already dim, the pines indistinct, and by the time he crossed the creek to where I was it was hard to find the trail. I sidestepped up the slope, planting my feet carefully, and I knew that it was an old man's way of climbing, my son waiting below me, watching, and I knew he was thinking that I moved too slowly, and he asked if I was OK.

At the truck we stripped off wet clothes and boots, packed our rods by flashlight, and headed back down the canyon. A half moon hung in the slot, orange from the smoke of Oregon fires that had burned all week. Geoff drove and the headlights swept the canyon walls and I drifted in and out of sleep.

IT IS NOVEMBER. The light has changed. Now it's a harder light and there is smoke in the air. The rice farmers are burning off the stubble so that the late sun burns orange. The river runs wide, sliding like oil in places, and near the bank there are salmon running, their dorsal fins showing as they roil in the shallows, surging up river. Wading into the river the current sucks at my legs, the water is black and as the sun sets along the levee, the boils where the salmon roll suddenly glow, then disappear. My fingers are numb, and Geoffrey, far out in the river, is no more than a lump blacker than the water. There is an egret along the far shore, white against the darkness, picking its way slowly. Overhead there are occasional snow geese. Earlier this afternoon on Agua Frias road, a long straight ruler that comes north from Butte City, rice fields, still not drained, were blanketed with snow geese, so many that it looked like a field of snow. Geoffrey says that in the morning when he's on the way to work they are restless, whirl up in great flocks that black out the sky.

Suddenly the line shudders and the rod bends but it's not a steelhead. I've snagged one of the salmon and I hold the rod steady, bending in an arc, while the line throbs. The salmon, perhaps twenty pounds, fins in the current, the dorsal fin out of the water, shrugs at the tension, slides off away from me into the current and there is nothing I can do. When it decides to go upstream the reel screams and then it is slack as the fly breaks off.

Now the river sucks at my legs, and behind me another salmon rolls. More are in front of me, sudden splashes with the sucking sound of big bodies halfway out of the water.

I make my way back to shore. Geoffrey will fish until it is too dark to see but I'm too old now to wade in the darkness. I'm remembering a hot afternoon when Art and I fished the West Branch, now under six hundred feet of water behind the Big Oro dam. We were high on the bank and we could see the dark torpedoes of salmon thrashing their way over the riffles, and in the long green pools females moving back and forth, digging redds with their tails.

Geoffrey and I drive back to Chico with only one headlight, startling a deer, an owl, jack rabbits, and meet Jill and the boys at a pizza parlor. My toes are still numb.

In the morning I drive up the canyon, following Geoff, Maria Callas rising in the cold air, and we fish at Pulga, and I start back down, the noon sun warming the truck, remembering October light and the hot sun, and plunging into a cold pool in the shadow of great granite slabs.

NEARLY FIFTY YEARS AGO, late in August, I was hired by Ginn and Co., a Boston educational publisher to travel to West Texas to talk to English teachers as part of their in-service program. Ginn flew me to Texas, rented a car for me and put me on the road to tiny high schools that played eight-man football and were in the middle of nowhere. Long, straight roads arrowed through miles of sagebrush and chaparral, the horizon flat and far off.

RATTLESNAKE ROUNDUP SEPT 9-11 a sign proclaimed near a store at the side of the two-lane highway. I stopped. When I stepped outside the car it felt as if I had stepped into an oven. Inside the store it was not any cooler.

What happens to the rattlesnakes that get captured, I asked the young man behind the counter.

"Some of them get released. Some of them are given to some folks what handles snakes. It's somewhere in the Bible." He paused. "Some of them get cooked."

"You ever eat any?"

"No. I never had no hankering for that."

I remembered Johnny, the cook at Feather River Camp cooking a rattlesnake for John Peterson and me late one night. John had captured the snake and kept it in camp so that the boys would know what the sound was like when it rattled. And now, at the end of the summer, Johnny cleaned it, cut it into small chunks and fried them.

"When I was a girl in Mississippi, we ate just about everything," she said. "Squirrels, rabbits, possum. And snakes."

John and I ate the tender pieces. It did not taste like chicken.

When I asked the Texas clerk if he had any sandwiches, he said, no. But he did have a loaf of bread that was so light it seemed to float in the air. A package of baloney and a small ketchup completed my lunch. That, and an ice-cold long-necked bottle of Lone Star beer. On the cooler was a bumper sticker that read, 'LONE STAR IS NO LONGER JUST A BREAKFAST DRINK.' There was a single small cottonwood next to the store. I sat at the old picnic table in the narrow shade. The only sound was the hum of the store's refrigeration, cooling the beer. The isolation was complete. What was I going to say to the three English teachers in the next town? I might just as well be arriving in a saucer, spiraling down from an alien planet. On an overpass near San Angelo, someone had painted, *This is not the end of the world but you can see it from here.* Far off was the horizon and if I looked long enough, it seemed to curve.

MY MOTHER and I drove out to the hospital to see my father. He was in an isolation ward, and could be viewed through a window. He raised one hand and waved at me. That's the last image I have of him. The tuberculosis swept through his lungs and he died.

"The Captain of all these men of death that came against him to take him down, was the consumption for it was that that brought him down to the grave," was how John Bunyon described it.

I was barely out of college. And I knew very little about the man who was my father. He left for the magic mountain in New Mexico when I was not yet ten. My mother took my two brothers and me to California to live with her aunt and uncle, and my father eventually returned, his case arrested (but later to return) when I went to high school, and he lasted until I graduated from the University of California. That was an important moment for him. It was not until years later, when my younger brother began to delve into the family history that I found out why it was such a milestone.

What did I know of the man? Almost nothing from him. Things came to me in bits and pieces from other people. I remember his slim figure, dressed in gabardine trousers and a white shirt. Once I saw him without the shirt and his concave chest was startling. They had collapsed one of his lungs in a sanitarium procedure, something that was supposed to let the lung rest and recover. But it was a kind of snake oil remedy.

He never struck me as frail. Perhaps it was because he seemed so positive, so determined to make the most of what was, in the 1950's a second-class status for a man. My mother went off to work and my father was the house-husband. He learned to cook. His meals were not particularly exiting, spaghetti and chicken in the pressure cooker, and casseroles that were heavy with tuna and cans of mushroom soup. He managed the household accounts in his meticulous hand, and spent time dealing with my younger brother's forays into academic forests. Paul wandered, and my father was determined to put him on a straight path, and he did. All three of us boys graduated from university. For my older brother there was no doubt. He was a genius at math and science and got a scholarship to the university. I got in by the skin of my teeth on what was then called a "principal's recommendation." But Paul was a project and my father managed to get him enrolled at Cal Poly when it was a small men-only university that specialized in agricultural studies.

Paul ended up as an engineer, I became a schoolteacher, and Ronald was a designer of main-frame computers in the days when those machines occupied whole rooms.

What else did I know about my father? Not much. But what do we know about our fathers? He was a mystery. He was blind in one eye as a result of an accident when I was an infant, and it wasn't until I was in my fifties and talking with my mother that she mentioned his glass eye. I was struck dumb, immediately called Paul to tell him, but he already knew. How blind had I been not to notice that one eye never moved? A draughtsman and a carpenter and cabinetmaker, he was meticulous in making things out of wood. There was a fence in the back yard on Regent Street and he instructed my younger brother and me as we cut the slats for the fence. We had to measure the wood to a sixty-fourth of an inch. "How wide is the kerf?" he asked. The kerf was the width of the teeth on the saw and only a cabinet maker would know that dimension. But it didn't matter whether it was a fence or a table destined for some expensive house in Berkeley, the width of the kerf was important. Of course, there weren't any tables bound for expensive houses in Berkeley. Only the fence in the back of the yard.

He shopped on College Avenue, made friends with a butcher and found out that the man owned a lot in east Oakland. It was a strange corner lot that dipped into a swale, and was thought to be unbuildable. But my father drew up the plans for a house that would fit into that bowl, and for the first time in his life he shepherded a house from plans to finish.

What else did I know about him? He had a job as a draftsman in a shipyard just outside of Chicago, working on plans for Liberty ships during WWII. He went to Willard Junior High to argue my younger brother's case against a tyrannical teacher. He lay in an isolation ward in a hospital in Oakland when the tuberculosis returned with a vengeance. I saw him through the window of that ward and he lifted his hand to wave at me. There was nothing else. No fishing expeditions, no games of catch on the sidewalk in front of the house, no talks about my future. The only time we ever touched that subject, I told him that I had been offered admission to Long Beach State College. It was a new California college, still in temporary buildings, and I was told that I would be a part of the track team. But he said no, it was a gamble that wasn't worth it, and if I went, there would be no support from either him or my mother. I felt devastated. But somehow he knew that it would not have worked out for me, that I would have been a pawn in someone else's game, and when the unexpected news came that I had been accepted by the University of California, he said nothing. Perhaps he paid attention to me in ways I didn't notice. I worked from two in the afternoon until ten at night throughout the week when I went to the University. I worked all day Saturday. I spent my summers in the Sierras working at the city of Oakland's summer camp. Our paths did not cross that much. He was a presence. I do not know if the enforced silence and inactivity of the sanatoriums changed him. He spent years in silent wards, lying in a bed or lying in the sun or sitting, reading (but never any books that were exciting!). I was the middle child, sandwiched between the brilliant scholar and the younger brother who rode motorcycles and got into trouble at school.

I think it was assumed that I would do all right. Often buried in a book as a child, I lived in a world filled with pirates and World War Two flying aces. In high school I was a determined runner and a part of the school newspaper. I cared nothing for math or science, was removed from chemistry for an unauthorized experiment that, the teacher said, could have caused serious damage to my classmates. But mostly I kept my nose clean and stayed out of the way of my parents. I was not afraid of my father. He was simply there.

My brother Paul, when he began to dredge the family records, found that my father had withdrawn from the University of Illinois in his senior year. All our lives we had believed that he had graduated, but there was the irrefutable proof that he had not earned a degree. Paul found his university records and discovered that he had taken boxing and fencing, a surprise to both of us. He had met my mother at the university and that connection was permanent, but his failure to graduate must have preyed on his mind. He leaned on us, and when we finally graduated, it must have been a release for him. He did not live long enough to see Paul graduate, but Paul was well on his way by then.

When he was in high school, Paul built a roadster, converting the frame of an old Ford, installing an engine. He built the car from the ground up even though he was still a high school student. What was unusual was that Paul, decades later, discovered that our father had taken courses in auto mechanics theory but he never talked with Paul about the building of the car, never came around to neighbor May Anderson's garage where Paul was buried in car parts and grease. As Paul put it, "He looked through the window." No visits to talk about what Paul was doing or why he was doing it. We were on our own.

What else did I know? Once, long after his death, I mentioned to my mother that he was a mild mannered man. "No," she said, "he could harbor deep anger. Once," she said, "he thought he would be unfairly fired from a job in Illinois and he carried his keys on a huge tractor nut for weeks. When the word came that he was to be let go, he planned to hurl the nut with his keys through the window on the boss's door. But that never happened," she said. When he was let go, the boss gave him a glowing recommendation.

I never heard him swear. His sense of humor was underplayed. Once, the boyfriend of our aunt Laura's friend, Ruth, was waiting at our house in Berkeley for her to show up. "I feel great today," he said. "I could lick my weight in tigers." The car pulled up to the curb and Ruth stepped out.

"Here comes your tiger," my father said to him.

I don't remember much else. I think my children have a better picture of their father than I have of mine. He grew up in an Illinois coal mining town but he never went down into the mines. Paul found a photograph of him in the woodshop at Hall Township High School. He stands in a white smock coat over his trousers and pressed shirt and tie, while the students pose with saws and drills, pretending to work while the photograph was taken.

I am about to turn seventy-nine. For fifty years, I taught school. Almost as long as he was alive. I have written a novel about a man with tuberculosis. The character is not my father. The only thing about that story that even vaguely resembles his life is a description of the little cottages at the Alum Rock Sanitarium in San Jose where he was for part of a year. Each little cottage contained four men, and the upper half of each side was screened. Big shutters could be cranked up to leave the cottage open to the air, and when they were up on a hot day, the cottage looked like a Chinese coolie's hat. At least I remember it that way. So I used that. Once he said that the sanitarium in New Mexico was "a place on the side of a mountain filled with men waiting to die." I used that, too, but nothing else. I didn't have much else that I could use. The novel, *Tom Hall*, is close to me. It is as if I accompanied him to that mountain where he lay motionless in a cottage with three other men, all of them suffering from a disease that would certainly end their lives. The story I wrote is fiction, but there are moments that are close to the truth. There is the sense of death that surrounds those who were, in a moment of bad luck, infected with TB. The Native Americans in that story are subject to the same inevitable doom, and it was what I found when I wandered in Arizona, looking for clues to my father's journey. "Red niggers," was the expression that I came across repeatedly. And I remembered the hope that my father, too, would find himself at the City of Hope in Southern California, a place that might return him to our family.

It is a story that is, I think, one that ought to find a widespread audience. It is a story of a boy who must deal with a life that has suddenly changed, and he must find the sense of what has happened to him.

And it is the story of the man who was part of my life and then, in an instant, was not.

WINSLOW HOMER PAINTED SUNRISE, Fishing in the Adirondacks in 1889. A year later the Nelson Creek bridge was built in a narrow canyon in the Sierra Nevada Mountains. Homer's painting shows a solitary man in a canoe on a lake, the water black, the ridge behind him such a dark green that it, too, is almost black. Above the ridge the clouds are tinged with red. Ten yards in front of his canoe a trout rises, a white circle in the black water. And halfway between the viewer's vantage point, the stance that Homer took in painting the scene, is another rise. We can barely see the fishing rod bent back in a false cast.

The narrow canyon below the Nelson Creek bridge is in shadow, the water dark green even at noon. The bridge is a web of rusted steel now, the plank boards of the roadway warped and twisted. I danced on that bridge once, the music coming from the open door of my truck parked on the road above the bridge. There must have been loons on Homer's lake, their plaintive cry echoing in the early morning light. In the Nelson Creek canyon there are stellar jays that shriek at intruders.

I remember watching a cast on Nelson Creek, the line snaking out, flat, reaching toward a pool that was on the other side of a race tumbling between granite boulders. Once, I fished that creek with my oldest son and when the light failed I came back to the trail that climbed up the wall of the canyon and waited. My son came out of the black and once again we sidestepped up the slope and when we reached the truck and slipped off our wet trousers and boots and leaned against the truck, I knew that I would not fish Nelson Creek many more times. I had reached the point where I would be better off in Winslow Homer's canoe, a dog at my feet, casting to the rise that was, to the fisherman, not much more than a sound in the dark.

I have returned again and again to that painting in the museum. I bought a postcard of the painting and have tacked it to the wall above my desk. I can imagine the silence of that morning, no wind, the lake flat and the trees still.

If the man in that canoe were in his mid-twenties, then he would have been my age in 1945 when I came west to California. I knew nothing about lakes or trout fishing or trout. But now, having passed eighty years, I know what it is like to walk in the narrow confines of a deep canyon and coax trout from a weed fringed pool, and the man in that canoe is familiar to me. I know him. I know the silence on that lake. I know how he feels as he casts to the rise of the trout that touches the surface in front of his canoe. I know the anticipation he feels as he watches the fly settle on the water.

I am there in that dark morning.